THE PERFECT DRINK
FOR EVERY OCCASION

THE PERFECT DRINK FOR EVERY OCCASION

151 COCKTAILS THAT WILL:
Freshen Your Breath,
Impress a Hot Date,
Cure a Hangover, and More!

BY DUANE SWIERCZYNSKI

QUIRK BOOKS
PHILADELPHIA

Library of Congress Cataloging in Publication Number: 2002094029

ISBN: 1-931686-29-7

Printed in Singapore
Typeset in Rotis Sans Serif and House Gothic

Design and icons by Susan Van Horn
Illustrations by Matt Madden

Distributed in North America by Chronicle Books
85 Second Street
San Francisco, CA 94105

10 9 8 7 6 5 4 3

Quirk Books
215 Church Street
Philadelphia, PA 19106
www.quirkbooks.com

*For Parker Lennon, who won't be allowed
to read this book until March 30, 2023.*

"I drink when I have occasion and sometimes when I have no occasion."

—MIGUEL DE CERVANTES

Contents

2. The Drink That Will Impress . . . _____ **47**

3. The Drink for Major Life Events _____ 65

6. The Perfect Time and Season _____127

Introduction

> *"Do not allow children to mix drinks. It is unseemly and they use too much vermouth."* —Steve Allen

Most of what I've learned about drinking has been accidental.

There was that time in college when I was 19 and trying desperately not to get carded at a jazz club in Philadelphia. I tried to think of the most adult drink imaginable, something that would make the waitress believe I was a 25-year-old hard bop aficionado, not some underaged joker. After much deliberation to the wailing sax of a John Coltrane tune, I came up with the answer. "Vodka and cranberry juice," I ordered proudly. The waitress rolled her eyes. I was shut down faster than a restaurant with a rat problem. I never heard the end of that Coltrane tune.

A few years later, I was nursing a miserable summer cold. In some fevered fugue state I recalled my grandfather Lou's age-old advice about how Southern Comfort—at least I think it was Southern Comfort—when mixed with warm honey and a squeeze of lemon juice—was it lemon juice?—would ease the symptoms of any cold. Being a bachelor, I didn't have any honey or lemon juice. (And I didn't think a silver packet of Ramen Noodle flavoring would do the trick.) So I skipped the fancy add-ons and had a shot of SoCo, neat. Bad move. Not only did the SoCo not ease any of my symptoms, it added a completely new one: extreme nausea.

I could go on and on. Years later still—when I finally thought I knew something about the world and my place in it—I stopped by a co-worker's Halloween party. My co-worker had a good 30 years on me; she was a respected veteran of the industry. So I decided against showing up in a costume. Excellent move on my part: Everyone at the party—who had, collectively, a good 492 years on me—was dressed in tasteful, casual evening wear. I was feeling very pleased with myself until someone asked me what I'd like to drink. "I'd love a beer," I said. "A beer?" asked my hostess, with a hint of sadness and quite possibly pity. "I don't think we—George, do we have beer? I don't think we have beer. My son Robert used to drink beer, but we haven't had any around the apartment for a while now. . . ." As I waited to be shown to the Little Kids' Table, I realized that I'd worn a Halloween costume after all: pre-professional loser.

The thing is, everything I've learned about drinking, I've learned the hard way. If only there had been a book that could have tipped me off in advance, I could have avoided these tough lessons. If only there were—oh I don't know—some handy, witty, affordably priced hardback book published by Quirk Books ($14.95, ISBN 1-931686-29-7) that laid out a series of perfect drinks for every possible occasion, things might have been different for me. For instance, I would have known what to order when underage in a fancy bar (see page 69), or the proper cocktail to relieve a cold (see page 34), or even what to order to impress your elders (see pages 50–53).

Fortunately, things will be different for you. That's because you, my friend, are holding a copy of *The Perfect Drink for Every Occasion* in your hands. (Note: If the above paragraph is missing or blacked out with a marker, that's because someone bought this book for you as a gift and doesn't want you to know how much he/she spent. Too bad—it was $14.95. Cheap!)

The Perfect Drink is the MacGyver of booze books: a truly handy tool that can bail you out of virtually any social situation with only a bottle of Absolut, some chewing gum, and six inches of string. How many times have you stood at a bar, wanting to try something new, but not knowing where to start? Or tried to impress someone with a trendy cocktail-of-the-moment but ended up ordering what you always order? Or been on tour with Don Rickles and he asks you to shake him up something, you blithering moron? These kinds of situations crop up all of the time. With *The Perfect Drink*, you'll always have your (gl)ass covered.

When I started writing this book, I vowed not to make yet another boring cocktail guide. Many drink recipe books are simply lists, with no context, no history, no rationale, and certainly no humor. (Unless you're the kind of person who giggles when you read the words "Sloe Comfortable Screw.") What good is that? Who ever opened up a drink recipe book at random and said, "Hmmm, gee, that Saskatoon Stinger sure sounds interesting. I believe I'll try me a tumbler of that!" No. You learn about a new drink when you're out at a bar and a friend orders something interesting, because there's almost always a cool story behind the drink. Or you learn about a new drink when you're traveling and order an exotic native delight. Or you learn about a new drink when you're dating someone new and you're introduced to his or her favorite tipple. So consider *The Perfect Drink* to be your new best friend, or even an exotic vacation, of sorts. (Just don't consider this book to be your new lover—behavior like that is prohibited in most states.)

I hope you enjoy *The Perfect Drink* and can avoid some of the stupid mistakes I've made and maybe even learn a little something about cocktails and responsible drinking. Which reminds me of the most important drinking lesson of all: Booze isn't the answer to everything.

But you know, it really does make the question seem less important.

CONVERTING MEASUREMENTS

If you're mixing a White Russian (p. 93) in Moscow or anywhere else in the metric world, a splash is still a splash. As for the rest, well, here's the math:

1 teaspoon = 5 milliliters	1 ounce = 30 milliliters
1 tablespoon = 15 milliliters	1 cup = nearly 1/4 liter

A Note on Chasers

You'll find mini-sidebars scattered throughout this book, paired with the appropriate drink. They come in three varieties:

 THE DRINK TO AVOID IN THIS SITUATION: Booze no-nos. Just as there are perfect drinks for every occasion, there are some downright hideous choices for these occasions, too. Drinking the wrong cocktail can result in injury, death, a jail term in the Deep South, deportation, and/or a really embarrassing tattoo on a sensitive part of your body. Take our advice and just say no to these.

THE PERFECT DRINKING GAME FOR THIS SITUATION: Like vermouth, drinking games should be used sparingly. But sometimes a particular occasion requires a suitable diversion. Like any event with your mother-in-law in attendance.

MIX IT RIGHT: These notes on specific liquors, garnish, and/or technique can vastly improve your drink. But if you're already mixing your fourth or fifth cocktail, you can pretty much skip these suckers.

The Perfect Set-Up

If you have a faithful manservant to cater to your every whim, you don't need to read this section. In fact, you don't even need to read this book; please hand this copy to your manservant. But the rest of you should pay careful attention. This chapter details the building blocks of every superfine cocktail in the world.

THE MAIN SPIRITS

Here are the King Daddy spirits, the Big Six, the cornerstones of nearly every mixed drink known to civilized man. Without 'em, you really don't have a cocktail. One word of advice: buy the best stuff you can afford. Never, ever stoop to buying the "rail" (a.k.a. cheapest) booze. If you spring for the top of the line hooch, you'll be rewarded with every sip.

BRANDY. They say she's a fine girl—what a good wife she would be. But brandy is also a spirit distilled from fruit or wine then aged in oak barrels. (The name comes from the Dutch word brandewijn, meaning "burnt wine.") Most American brandy comes from wine and is made in California. **Cognac** is the finest form of brandy and—like its snooty cousin Champagne—can only come from a legally defined region in France surrounding the town of Cognac. Time is everything with Cognac, which comes in three ages: V.S. (Very Superior), meaning the Cognac was aged two to three years; V.S.O.P. (Very Superior Old Pale), aged between four-and-a-half and six years; and X.O. (Extremely Old), which is aged more than six-and-a-half years—sometimes as many as 40. Some popular brands include Remy Martin, Hennessy, and Courvoisier, the latter of which is also a Busta Rhymes song. The lesser-known cousin of Cognac is **armagnac**, only this is distilled in a different part of France.

But that's not all. Italian brandy is sometimes known as **grappa**. Greek brandy is called **ouzo**. Turkish and Syrian brandy is **raki**. Some popular fruit brandies include **applejack**, **calvados**, and **framboise**. Brandy is known as a universal healer, which is why those big burly rescue dogs carry it in barrels around their necks.

GIN. Introduced in the mid-1700s, gin quickly became England's national drink. In the words of *GQ* drinks columnist Terry Sullivan: "Gin hit London the way crack hit the Bronx." It's pretty much vodka, but gin has been distilled again with juniper berries and a bunch of other botanicals (coriander, angelica root, cassia bark, lemons, oranges, what-ever) to give each different brand its distinctive taste. Never ask for just a "gin and tonic" at a bar, or you'll be served the rail gin, which is infused with the lowest quality of botanicals. And there's no hangover worse than a rail gin hangover. When you die and go to hell, the Devil himself will hand you a rail gin Martini and chuckle to Himself, deeply in His throat.

RUM. Drinkers have long referred to rum as "the demon," and anyone who's ever gotten sick from one too many Rum and Cokes knows why. It's distilled from molasses, the byproduct of refining sugar, and comes in three styles: light (or white), gold (amber), or dark. The British Navy used to prescribe it to their sailors for scurvy. But nobody—including the British Navy—knows where the word "rum" comes from. One theory has it that it comes from saccharum, the Latin word for sugar. Here's another conundrum: if a "rummy" is someone who drinks too much rum, what the hell is a "gin rummy?"

TEQUILA. The only popular spirit to have a 1950s rock instrumental named after it. (Sing it together: *"Ba-da-da-da-dah-dah-bum, Tequila!"*) Tequila is distilled from the heart of the blue agave plant, which only sounds like it comes from *The Lord of the Rings;* in truth, it's actually a relative of the lily. Like Cognac, tequila is tequila only when it comes from a particular geographic region—in this case, Jalisco, Mexico. Every other blue agave distilled spirit is called **mezcal**. Never buy a bottle of tequila with a dead worm in it—it's a lame marketing ploy and those little wriggly suckers don't add one iota of flavor. Though they are nice and chewy.

VODKA. Seemingly the Barry Manilow of booze: tasteless, odorless, and without distinctive character or flavor. It's distilled from grain and occasionally the random potato or two. Vodka began life in the States as a punch line to a Russian joke (one recipe from the 1930s called for the drinker to "tossitoff quickski") only to become the most beloved spirit in America. Vodka is also the stealth bomber of booze: capable of flying below the radar in almost every terrain and strong enough to annihilate sobriety with extreme prejudice. Some people think that vodka—which looks so neat and clean—is incapable of giving its drinker a hangover, but that is not true. Oh, boy is that not true.

WHISKEY. A spirit distilled from grain and aged in oak casks. If it has an "e," that means it came from the United States or Ireland. No "e"? Scotland or Canada. (If the name of the country has an "e" in it, so does the whiskey.) Let's tackle the American versions first. **Bourbon** is distilled from corn (at least 51 percent) and by order of the United States government, can only be made in the United States—in Bourbon County, Kentucky, to be precise. **Rye** is distilled from at least 51 percent rye, the rest being barley and corn. **Corn whiskey** these days is typically known as moonshine and was the basis of the Whiskey Rebellion of 1792, which erupted when the government first tried to tax booze. It's made with 80 percent corn and 20 percent barley and rye. Moving north, most **Canadian whisky** is blended and uses rye as its base. Hopping across the pond, **Irish whiskey** is a blend of barley malt and assorted grains. And **Scotch** is pretty much Irish whiskey, except that the malt is burned over peat fires, which imparts a smoky flavor.

LIQUEURS, WINES, APERITIFS, AND OTHER ADD-ONS

Liqueurs are the helpful sidekicks to a cocktail that can also occasionally be enjoyed by themselves. Just remember: there's a reason you don't see too many people curled up with a brown bag-wrapped bottle of crème de cacao. *Wines* are made from fermented grapes and have been enjoyed by humans from at least 7000 B.C. until late last night. *Aperitif* is a fancy French word meaning "to open," and refers to pre-dinner drinks that whet the appetite. Then again, some aperitifs have the opposite effect, so what do the French know? *Other add-ons* include all of the other bizarre things that human beings have chosen to ferment and market over the years, such as Southern Comfort and schnapps. Some of these "proprietary" liquors contain secret ingredients that the manufacturer refuses to reveal, a la the secret sauce on a McDonald's Big Mac.

An asterisk (✳) denotes the most common add-ons, which are worth picking up if you'd like to mix many of the cocktails in this book.

AMARETTO. This is the Italian word for "a little bitter." Appropriately enough, this is a bitter Italian liqueur tempered with almonds and apricots. A favorite of the Godfather's.

✳BAILEY'S IRISH CREAM. This liqueur contains fresh dairy cream, but eerily enough, you never have to refrigerate it—the Irish whiskey inside keeps the cream preserved.

BENEDICTINE. Here's one of those liqueurs with a secret formula, which has been kept locked in a vault since monks in Normandy first concocted this spirit in the sixteenth century. However, one of those monks must have gotten drunk one night because we do know that Benedictine is based on Cognac, only sweeter.

*BITTERS.** The secret weapon of many cocktails, bitters are spirits with herbs, roots, spices, and other generally unidentifiable natural ingredients. Pharmacists originally experimented with bitters for medicinal purposes, but soon the concoction started to find its way into cocktails. (Forget sugar—a spoonful of Jack Daniel's always makes the medicine go down.) The most popular brand is the **Angostura** bitters, which was invented in 1830 by a Prussian surgeon named Dr. Johann Gottlieb Benjamin Siegert to fight malaria. Now his formula is made in Trinidad and conscripted to fight cocktail malaise. No home bar is complete without a bottle. Another type of bitters, **Peychaud's**, is essential in the New Orleans classic the Sazerac (see page 144). **Orange** bitters are nearly impossible to find, but were used extensively in many older drinks. Technically, **Jaegermeister** qualifies under the "bitters" heading, but many prefer to do shots with it.

CACHAÇA. A 500-year-old Brazilian spirit that's a close cousin to tequila, but distilled from sugar cane instead of the blue agave plant.

CALVADOS. Take apple juice, put it in an oak cask, and presto, you'll have this French apple brandy. Okay, maybe there's a bit more to it than that—for instance, you should be in Normandy and have about four years on your hands.

CAMPARI. In 1860, Gaspare Campari concocted this blend of booze, fruit, spices, and herbs to create his namesake aperitif, and he kept mum on the exact ingredients for the rest of his life. The Campari company continues to guard his secret to this day. Campari is deep red and about as bitter as the producers of *Lifetime: Television for Women*.

*CHAMBORD. A favorite of King Louis XIV, this French black raspberry liqueur is extremely sweet and can often be found fraternizing with vodka, coffee, cream, and even sake. The bottle is amazing: a bulbous squat thing done up in gold trim S&M gear, with locks and everything. It's worth buying for looks alone, but Chambord is a key ingredient in many cocktails.

*CHAMPAGNE. You know the drill by now—if the sparkling wine came from the Champagne region of France, it's Champagne. If it comes from somewhere else, it's just sparkling wine. If it comes in a brown paper bag, you're in trouble.

CHARTREUSE. Another cordial with a ton of—in this case, 130—secret herbs and spices. **Green chartreuse** (55 percent alcohol) is stronger than **yellow chartreuse** (40 percent alcohol). According to the Chartreuse Diffusion company, the Smithereens and Bon Jovi are big fans of this particular cordial (so was Jay Gatsby, who swilled some in chapter 5 of F. Scott Fitzgerald's most famous novel).

*COINTREAU. A brand-name fancy-pants form of triple sec. (See page 18.) This is an extremely popular cordial used in many cocktail recipes, probably thanks to its sweet-yet-bitter orange kick. The manufacturer alleges that it's made from European, African, and Caribbean orange peels. It also has a very cool bottle—squat and square, with rounded edges.

*CRÈME DE CACAO. A cordial made from cacao beans, which are grown largely in South America and Mexico and are an important ingredient in chocolate. And, like chocolate, crème de cacao comes in white and brown varieties. Since both taste the same, your choice should be based completely on looks.

CRÈME DE CASSIS. A French liqueur made from black currants and a host of other berries. The exact recipe is a carefully guarded secret of the manufacturer.

CRÈME DE MENTHE. A white or green liqueur made from concentrated mint leaves. To this day, no one has successfully invented a drink called "Crème de-Ment-ed." I think it's high time. The white stuff is premium; go for the green only when you're making something where a green hue is the desired effect.

⁕CURACAO. This form of triple sec may come from the Caribbean, but it bleeds American all the way through—it comes in red, white, and blue varieties. None are as sweet as other triple secs.

DRAMBUIE. A whiskey-based liqueur made with honey, assorted herbs, and Highland malt whiskeys that are like Jerry Lee Lewis's wives—at least 15 years old.

DUBONNET. A French wine fortified with wines and herbs. This aperitif was a big hit during Prohibition—among those who could find it, that is—because it masked the harsh taste of bad bathtub gin.

FRAMBOISE. A fruit brandy made from raspberries.

FRANGELICO. Wild hazelnuts, berries, flowers, and other secret ingredients. Yeah, it's another one of those mysterious "proprietary" liqueurs.

GALLIANO. A golden Italian liqueur made with over 80 herbs—including lavender, juniper, and anise. Many Galliano fans like to sip it after a big meal.

*****GRAND MARNIER.** A liqueur made with Cognac and laced with an orangey flavor. "Grand" also describes the price, but it's worth the purchase since it's the finishing touch on many classic drinks.

*****GRENADINE.** A sweet, blood-red syrup made from pomegranates that is used for both flavor and coloring. It is used in more cocktails than you can possibly imagine, from Shirley Temples to Zombies.

*****KAHLUA.** A coffee liqueur from *Meh-HEE-ko* that is distilled from sugar cane. Contrary to popular belief, there is no chocolate in Kahlua.

KIRSCHWASSER. A clear and dry fruit brandy distilled from cherries and cherry pits.

KUMMEL. A liqueur made from cumin, caraway seeds, and anise that tastes like spearmint.

LILLET. A French aperitif made partially with Bordeaux wine, Armagnac, and assorted herbs and fruits.

MARASCHINO. A tough-to-find Italian liqueur distilled from sour marasca cherries. Some mixologists treat Maraschino like water direct from Lourdes: a magical fluid with the ability to cure cancer, make the lame walk, and banish static cling from your socks. So if you see a bottle, pick it up. You'll probably be able to sell it to one of those nutty mixologists on eBay for a lot of money.

MIDORI. A Japanese spirit made from green honeydews.

ORGEAT. Almond-flavored syrup that is very handy in sweet, tropical drinks.

*PERNOD.** The next best thing to absinthe, and that's a good thing since real absinthe will make you crazy. The exact ingredients of Pernod (pronounced *pehr-NOH*) are a secret, but numerous plants and fennel oils are definitely in the mix. It's yellowish in color and tastes a bit like licorice. The French like to mix Pernod with ice and water as a cloudy sipping drink. Then again, the French love Jerry Lewis.

PORT. A Portuguese fortified wine that comes in three varieties: ruby, vintage, and tawny. It's usually served as a dessert drink, but some enterprising mixologists have found ways to include it in cocktails, too.

SAMBUCA. Dig licorice? You'll love this liqueur, which is primarily made of the stuff along with witch elderbush—technical name: *Sambucus Nigra.*

SCHNAPPS. "Schnapp" is German for "snap," but it should actually translate to "schweet." American schnapps are a relatively new phenomenon and every year seems to bring a new fruit or candy flavor: peach, peppermint, butterscotch, root beer, and even cranberry.

SLOE GIN: This liqueur is flavored with a wild European plum known as a sloe.

SOUTHERN COMFORT. Still another proprietary brand with a host of "secret ingredients," which may or may not be bourbon, brandy, peaches, and other assorted herbs.

*TRIPLE SEC.** This is not Brooklyn-ese for "three seconds." The words translate into "triple dry," meaning that this orange liqueur was distilled three times. It's the poor man's Cointreau.

VERMOUTH. Vermouth is fortified wine infused with herbs and spices, but it all depends on the country of origin. French vermouth is dry and white (and typically referred to as "dry vermouth"), while Italian vermouth is sweet and red (and referred to as "sweet vermouth"). Some Martini drinkers have a love/hate relationship with dry vermouth—they love to complain about how much they would hate even a drop of the stuff in their precious gin or vodka.

WINE: Grapes that have been allowed to ferment turn into alcohol. Most people mistakenly think that white wine comes from green grapes and red wine from red grapes. All grapes are "white" on the inside—red wine results from combining the red skins with the rest of the fermenting grape. Popular white wines include Chardonnay, Pinot Grigio, and Chablis. Popular reds include Merlot, Cabernet, and Shiraz.

MIXERS AND GARNISHES

Just as opium requires a den, a Martini requires an olive. Most cocktails aren't cocktails without the perfect mixers or garnishes—simple non-alcoholic beverages or fruit that can single-handedly save a drink from tasting like a glass full of gasoline.

MIXERS. Tonic water, ginger ale, lemon-lime soda, club soda, cola and diet cola, cranberry juice, orange juice, lime juice, lemon juice, grapefruit juice, tomato juice, and pineapple juice.

GARNISHES. Olives, orange slices, maraschino cherries, limes, lemons, cucumbers, and celery. The fresher, the better. In fact, the perfect cocktail party begins with a trip to the farmer's market or produce shop and then to your local liquor emporium.

THE HARDWARE

In college you could get away with a single shot glass and a plastic sleeve full of Solo cups. If you were running a fancy joint, you'd add a plastic beer funnel and a baking tin to hold the Jell-O shots. But now it's time to put away such childish things. No adult bar should be without the following:

SHAKER

A device used to mix cocktail ingredients with ice, thereby chilling the bejesus out of them. You have two choices: the Boston variety, which consists of a mixing glass and a metal cup that overlaps the glass; or a standard shaker, which looks like something out of the *Apollo* lunar missions. The pros prefer the Boston variety, mainly for speed.

MARTINI PITCHER

For when you want something stirred, not shaken—and technically, Martinis fall into this category.

STRAINER

The bartending tool that looks like a spare part from *RoboCop*. The coiled spring is meant to hold back the ice, yet allow some of the pulp and foam of the cocktail through to the glass.

JIGGER

The bartending tool that looks like a silver egg cup. One end holds 1½ ounces, a.k.a. a "jigger," or one regulation-sized shot. The other end holds exactly 1 ounce, a.k.a. a "pony."

BAR SPOON

A thin long-handled spoon used to mix cocktails. Some have a flat end that can be used instead of a muddler (see below).

MUDDLER

Used to crush the bejesus out of fruit, herbs, and annoying guests who flirt with your date. Fancier muddlers are a miniature bowl and bat combination, like a mortar and pestle.

JUICER

Many of the drinks in this book call for fresh fruit juice. Won't the bottled/canned/frozen stuff do? Don't ever say that in front of a mixologist, or he'll beat you about the face and neck. Any cocktail—even a Screwdriver—is vastly improved if you use fresh fruit and a handheld juicer.

ICE BUCKET AND TONGS

Only losers run to the freezer for ice—and then use their paws to scoop it out of the trays. Grow up, already.

ICE CRUSHER

Big, clunky Fisher-Price–sized blocks of ice say "amateur home mixologist"; frosty scoops of finely crushed ice say, "Trust me, sweetheart, I know what I'm doing."

SPEED POURERS

Consider it "speed dial" for the tops of your most-used bottles of booze.

BOTTLE STOPPERS

Don't want to be screwing around all night? Buy a handful of decorative stoppers and deploy them in your most popular bottles.

OTHER ITEMS TO HAVE ON HAND. A cutting board, blender, colored toothpicks, a good corkscrew, wine bottle stoppers (VacuVin rubber stoppers, complete with pump, are terrific), paring knife, swizzle sticks, napkins, and coasters.

THE GLASSWARE

As every backside needs its own style of denim jean, every drink demands its own comfortable cradle. Patrick Gavin Duffy's *The Official Mixer's Manual* from 1948 details no less than 30 individual drinking vessels, but you can get away with a few of the basics.

COCKTAIL GLASS

 The classic V-shaped glass that has become shorthand for "boozing it up." Typically, these hold 3½ ounces. Cocktail glasses that hold 4 ounces are known as martini glasses.

OLD FASHIONED GLASS

Synonymous with "rocks glass." To the untrained eye, this simply looks like a tumbler. Find one (or four) that holds 6 to 8 ounces. A double rocks glass holds 15 to 16 ounces.

COLLINS GLASS

About as ordinary a piece of barware as you'll ever find; it looks suspiciously like a regular drinking glass, except perhaps smaller or thinner. This bad boy should hold 10 to 14 ounces.

HIGHBALL GLASS

Like a collins glass, only squatter and wider. These should hold 8 ounces.

PILSNER GLASS

 The classiest beer vessel imaginable, save a monstrous German beer stein held aloft by two leggy models. Typically, pilsners hold 10 to 12 ounces—one regular-sized bottle or can of beer.

PINT GLASS

 Like you don't know what I'm talking about.

WHITE WINE GLASS

 There are a million varieties of white wine glasses, which can hold anywhere from 5 to 10 ounces. Look for something on the smaller side, with thin glass and crisp, elegant edges. White wines, such as a fine California Chardonnay, shouldn't be served in a vessel more suited for a Cherry Slurpee.

RED WINE GLASS

 Typically, red wine glasses have wider bowls so the wine can breathe. (Apparently, white wine can hold its breath.) They also come in sizes ranging from 5 to 10 ounces. Go for something larger and with thicker glass.

CHAMPAGNE FLUTE/GLASS

 The flutes—which are European in origin—are specially shaped to preserve as many bubbles as possible. (They also launch easily and forcefully into a blazing fireplace.) Look for one that holds about 7$\frac{1}{2}$ ounces. The American version looks like a cocktail glass, only much shallower and wider. Screw the American version and stick with a flute.

SNIFTER

 The oversized bowl—which can hold anywhere from 5 to 25 ounces—and stumpy little stem wasn't designed for its holder to look snooty; instead, the warmth of your hand is supposed to warm the brandy or Cognac inside.

POUSSE-CAFÉ AND PARFAIT GLASSES

 Glassware with a straight bowl and no tapering. These are especially handy for layering different kinds of booze on top of each other. Parfait glasses are usually larger than pousse-café glasses.

MARGARITA GLASS

A very distinctive piece of glassware that some say resembles a sombrero turned upside down. To line the tops of a glass with salt, simply run a lime wedge along the rim, then dip the glass into a plate of coarse table salt. (If you don't drink enough Margaritas to justify the purchase a set of four, a nice red wine glass will do nicely, too.)

SHOT GLASS

The first thing you ever purchased at the campus bookstore.

The Perfect Technique

There are countless classes and books dedicated to teaching the art of combining spirits, liqueurs, wines, mixers, and garnishes. I'm going to distill all of these lessons down to about 60 seconds. Hang on.

HOW TO POUR BOOZE

The essence of every drink, of course, is to transport the booze from its original bottle into another vessel. Traditionally, this is known as pouring. But you can't just go tipping one end up and hoping for the best. Drink recipes are delicate things. Here are three ways to make sure you don't pour too little or too much.

1. THE JIGGER

This is where you actually use bar tools to accurately and safely measure each and every lousy shot. For losers and bartenders at T.G.I. Friday's only. Let's move on.

2. THE TWO FINGERS

Need to pour 1½ ounces of booze and don't want to play around with one of those jigger deals? Some pros use the two fingers method. Wrap your index and middle fingers around the bottom of the glass and stop pouring when the level reaches the tops of your fingers. If you're Calista Flockhart, you can go a little over your finger mark. If you're John Goodman, a little below. Experiment. You'll get it right. Or very drunk.

3. THE COUNT

Most bartenders, however, use the count method. First, you need one of those speed pourers—the silver tops that fit onto your bottles and guide the booze into a nice, consistent stream, otherwise it would splash all over your shirt. Next, fill an empty bottle of booze with tap water, then fill a highball glass two-thirds of the way with ice. Now pour the water into the glass, with the bottle completely upside-down—none of that half-assed, tilted-part-of-the-way stuff. As the water is pouring, count off in your head: one one thousand, two one thousand, three one thousand, stop. Roughly, you should have poured an ounce and a half. Check your measurements and try again and again until your counting matches the flowing water. (Why do you think you're using water?) This is extremely impressive to the opposite sex, especially those still attending high school.

MEASURES OF SUCCESS

Just in case you're anal about exactly how much booze goes into your drink, here's a handy reference guide to translate recipe measurements (dashes, teaspoons, etc.) into cold, hard ounces.

MEASUREMENT	OUNCES	MEASUREMENT	OUNCES
1 splash	1/16	1 medium lemon	1 1/2
1 dash	1/8	1/4 cup	2
1 teaspoon	1/6	1/2 cup	4
1 tablespoon	1/2	1 cup	8
1 pony	1	1 pint	16
1 medium lime	1	1 quart	32
1 jigger	1 1/2		

HOW TO COMBINE IT

Now that you've learned the three ways to pour booze, here are the three basic ways to combine it with other spirits, liqueurs, mixers, or ice.

TECHNIQUE #1: STIR

James Bond was a moron. You should never shake a Martini, or any other clear, thin liquids for that matter. Doing so will make your drink cloudy. Instead, simply add the parts of the drink to an ice-filled glass (filled either two-thirds of the way, or to the rim) and put that stirrer, be it a swizzle stick or screwdriver, to work. You can get fancy about it—some bartenders in high-end hotel bars have been known to give their Martinis no less than 100 stirs—or just whip that swizzle stick around the glass a couple of times. Some drinks require that you mix the ingredients in a separate container, then strain the result into your glass; others let you stir the ingredients in the glass. As in brain surgery, it helps to follow the directions.

TECHNIQUE #2: SHAKE

Shaking is for more complex, thicker ingredients, like fruit juice. Never shake a drink containing soda or carbonated water. If you've ever shaken a cocktail before, you may have noticed the vacuum effect—difficulty removing the shaker lid/glass. And once you do wrench it free, some of the cocktail ends up on your khakis. For a standard shaker, simply give it one last downward shake, snapping your wrist a bit, which should help break the seal. For the Boston variety, look for the moisture line on the silver cup (this tells you where the glass meets silver). Tap it gently, which should loosen things up.

As for further shaking technique, I like to take my cues from Nick Charles, the dipsomaniacal private eye from Dashiell Hammett's classic *The Thin Man* (1934). For Nick, the rhythm is everything: "Always have rhythm in your shaking," he says. "Now a Manhattan you always shake to fox-trot time, a Bronx to two-step time, a dry Martini you always shake to waltz time."

TECHNIQUE #3: BLEND

The Black & Decker method. Hardly any work at all—you have the electric company doing the heavy lifting. Blending is best for exotic Polynesian drinks, not-so-exotic frozen concoctions like the Margarita, and getting rid of evidence.

① THE DRINK THAT WILL . . .

> *"If your doctor warns that you have to watch your drinking, find a bar with a mirror."* –John Mooney

We ask a lot of our drinks. We want them to help us celebrate, pat us reassuringly on the back, give us the nerve to walk up to someone, perk up an otherwise boring business lunch, and generally keep us company. But you probably didn't know that certain drinks are capable of so much more. In fact, when mixed properly, some drinks can even . . .

THE PERFECT DRINK

Freshen Your Breath

 VODKA AND CRANBERRY

This is not meant to replace your morning shot of Listerine, of course. But it is helpful to know which drinks make your breath more pleasing to the opposite sex when you're at a cocktail party. In general: anything with citrus, gin, and/or vodka—for example, a Gimlet, a Gin and Tonic, a Gin Fizz—will keep your breath alive.

MIXOLOGY

1 1/2 oz. vodka

Cranberry juice

Fill a collins glass two-thirds of the way with ice, pour in the vodka, and then add the cranberry juice to fill. Stir briskly.

THE DRINK TO AVOID IN THIS SITUATION: Beer. You should also avoid drinks containing milk, and anything as cloyingly sweet as your high school prom date.

Help You Lose Weight

 LIGHT RUSSIAN

Are you pounding White Russians like the Commies are still a global superpower? Ditch the vodka (and the 150 calories found in two ounces of the stuff) and substitute the crème de cacao—it'll taste practically the same. Okay, maybe it's not exactly something you'd find at Jenny Craig, but it's certainly better than dumping rum into your Slim Fast shake.

MIXOLOGY

1 1/2 oz. Kahlua

4 oz. skim milk

1 splash white crème
de cacao

*Fill a collins glass
two-thirds of the way with ice, pour in the
ingredients, and stir.*

Relieve Your Cold

 SNOOTER ROOTER

The secret ingredient here? Surprisingly, not the tomato juice. It's the Tabasco and horseradish, which contain nasal congestion-clearing agents (capsaicin and allyl isothiocyanate, respectively). You'll be breathing easy in no time.

MIXOLOGY

1 oz. vodka	2 dashes Worcestershire sauce
5 oz. tomato juice	5 shakes black pepper
1 tsp. lemon juice	1 1/2 tsp. horseradish
10 drops Tabasco sauce	Lime slice

Shake everything but horseradish and lime with ice, then strain over ice in a highball glass. Garnish with horseradish and lime.

THE DRINK TO AVOID IN THIS SITUATION: Milk-based drinks such as White Russians and Kahlua and Creams, which will only give your nose more ammo—hey, wait a second! You're supposed to be sick. Head home and rest already.

Relax Your Belly
After a Huge Meal

 SGROPPINO AL LIMONE

Can't believe you ate the whole thing? Try this Italian "unknotter"—that's what "sgroppino" means, more or less. If Dean Martin were forced at gunpoint to eat sorbet, this is what he'd order.

MIXOLOGY

1 oz. vodka

1 1/2 oz. lemon sorbet

2 oz. crushed ice

Blend all three for 20 seconds on the highest setting in a blender. Serve in a Champagne flute. You can also substitute vanilla ice cream and fresh lemon juice (to taste) for the sorbet.

Bust Up a Gallstone

 GALL IN THE FAMILY

Did Papa have a rolling gallstone? Avoid a piece of the rock by sipping this drink, along with another two cups of joe every day. Researchers at the Harvard School of Public Health found that guys who slugged down two or three cups of coffee every day had a 40 percent lower risk of gallstones. The study author, Michael Leitzmann, M.D., theorized that the high levels of caffeine can help the gallbladder get rid of the cholesterol that helps form those nasty little stones.

MIXOLOGY

1¹/₂ oz. Bailey's Irish Cream

5 oz. coffee

Pour the booze into a steaming hot cup of joe.

MIX IT RIGHT: Would you serve ice cold beer in a steaming pint glass right out of the dishwasher? Of course not. So never serve a hot drink in an ice-cold mug. Simply run hot water from the tap over the mug and pat dry. Thick earthenware mugs are best, since they retain heat longer.

Take the Pain Away

 BLUE CURE

Not the pain of the unending nightmare that is your stinking, miserable life. We mean the pain of stiff muscles from working out too hard or being cramped in a cubicle all week. The curacao contains orange peel, which contains a phytochemical called "hesperidin" believed to soothe inflamed muscles. The quinine in the tonic water has long been considered a cure for cramped muscles. The ounce of vodka won't hurt ya, either.

MIXOLOGY

1 oz. blue curacao   1 splash lime juice

1 oz. vodka   Sprite

1/2 oz. tonic water   Pineapple slice

Pour the blue curacao, vodka, tonic water, and lime juice into an ice-filled collins glass, then fill with Sprite. Stir three times, then add the pineapple slice.

THE DRINK TO AVOID IN THIS SITUATION: Red wine, which some researchers claim has a substance that negates the alcohol's calming effect. Plus, the sulfites in red wine have been known to trigger a migraine in some drinkers.

Settle Your Stomach

CALM AFTER THE STORM

Got that not-so-peaceful, queasy feeling? Forget the Alka-Seltzer and try this drink, which has two ingredients working in your favor: the red wine contains tummy-settling compounds, and the pineapple juice has an enzyme called bromelain, also proven to calm upset stomachs.

MIXOLOGY

1 1/2 oz. port wine

3 oz. pineapple juice

Club soda

Lemon twist

Shake the wine and juice with ice and strain into a highball glass with ice. Top with club soda, then garnish with lemon twist.

Decrease Your Risk of Heart Attack

 THE DEFIBRILLATOR

The benefits of the French paradox, all without having to put up with any annoying Frenchmen. The orange juice in this drink will raise your levels of good cholesterol (HDL), while the red wine will reduce the risk of blood clots and lower your bad cholesterol.

MIXOLOGY

2 oz. Dubonnet Rouge

4 oz. orange juice

Maraschino cherries

Shake with ice and strain into a highball glass with ice.

Garnish with cherries.

Get a Woman to Have Sex with You

 LIQUOR ALL OVER

No, it isn't fire that's going to work magic here—it's the Sambuca. According to Alan R. Hirsch, M.D., a researcher at the Smell and Taste Treatment and Research Foundation in Chicago and author of *Scentsational Sex*, licorice is a smell that many women associate with sexual arousal and can increase vaginal blood flow up to 13 percent.

MIXOLOGY

1 1/2 oz. Sambuca   Lime wedge

1/2 oz. gin

Mix both liquids in snifter and ignite with match. Extinguish the flames with a saucer. Serve with lime wedge.

MIX IT RIGHT: With any flaming drink, you should let it burn only a few seconds. (In other words, don't break out the sticks and marshmallows.) Burn it too long and you'll burn away all of the alcohol.

THE DRINK TO AVOID IN THIS SITUATION: Anything that smells like cherries. Dr. Hirsch found that blood flow dropped 18 percent when he opened up a jar of maraschinos.

Get a Man to Have Sex with You

 BLUE MOON PUMPKIN ALE

As for men, the scent that really got the ol' penile blood flowing—up to 40 percent—was the scent of pumpkin. (Blue Moon is just one of many microbreweries who make a pumpkin-based ale.) The other top scent was lavender, but it's impossible to find a beer or cocktail made with lavender. And that's probably a good thing.

MIXOLOGY

Blue Moon Brewing Company is actually owned by beer giant Coors, but don't let that stop you. If your local supermarket or beer distributor doesn't carry Blue Moon Pumpkin Ale, contact the company directly at 5151 East Raines Road; Memphis, Tennessee; 38118; 901-325-2000.

Help You Survive a Sinking Ship

 WHISKEY

Charles Joughin was the bakery chef on a little-known transatlantic ship called the *Titanic*. When the ship played chicken with an iceberg and lost, Joughin wasn't lucky enough to make it into a raft. But he was lucky enough to be rotund and drunk on whiskey, which kept him warm and afloat in the 28-degree water. He was the only passenger to survive in the water, and that's largely thanks to the booze.

MIXOLOGY

1 bottle of strong whiskey

1 sinking ship

As soon as you hear that an iceberg has ripped a gash in the hull, start doing shots of your whiskey. If you see Leonardo DiCaprio, use him as a flotation device.

Make You Smarter

STROKE OF GENIUS

Some researchers believe that a combination of caffeine and booze can help your brain tissue bounce back after an injury, such as a stroke. Researchers at the University of Texas tried the theory out on a bunch of rats who had suffered strokes and found that the rats who had a caffeine/alcohol cocktail had significantly less brain damage. If anyone asks why you're using Maker's Mark instead of Jack Daniel's, tell them it blends better and is slightly sweeter, which will make you sound smarter already.

MIXOLOGY

4 oz. Maker's Mark bourbon

6 oz. Coca-Cola

Fill a cocktail glass with ice, pour in the Maker's Mark, then mix in the Coke to taste.

Make You Go Insane

 ABSINTHE OF MALICE

There's a reason the French—and later, the rest of the civilized world—banned absinthe (a.k.a. "The Green Curse") in 1915. Absinthe is the crack of the booze world. It's potent, lethal, habit-forming, and passed out freely at the gates of hell. The lethal component is wormwood, which contains a mild hallucinogenic that made it very popular among writers and artists at the end of the nineteenth century, including Van Gogh, Degas, Whitman, Thackeray, and Wilde. But when combined with alcohol, wormwood can turn deadly and lead to convulsions and lesions on the brain. The only places you can buy a real bottle of absinthe are England, Spain, Portugal, and the Czech Republic. Some thrill-seekers attempt to make their own version with wormwood, vodka, fennel seeds, anise seeds, cardamom, and angelica root. Need I repeat myself? *Lesions on the brain*, folks.

MIXOLOGY

5 oz. absinthe

Pour the absinthe over crushed ice and prepare to see visions undreamed of in all of mankind . . . and later, your toilet.

44

Make You Go Only Slightly Insane

 ABSINTHE DRIP FRAPPE

If you're curious about the Green Muse but would rather stay on this side of reality, you might consider this tamed-down version, with a popular absinthe substitute called Pernod. Same weird, bitter taste, but no visit to an asylum required.

MIXOLOGY

2 oz. Pernod

1 sugar cube

Club soda

This takes some effort. First, fill a tumbler with crushed ice. Toss in the Pernod and place the sugar cube on top. Slowly drip club soda onto the sugar cube until it is completely melted away. Mix it well, then strain it into a cocktail glass.

Kill the Slugs in Your Backyard

 ## A REALLY CHEAP CAN OF BEER

For reasons known only to God, garden-variety slugs are extremely fond of beer. They don't care if it's a pint of Stella Artois from a Belgian restaurant or if it's a dead solider left over from a 1978 frat party. They'll go for the brew, then drown in it. Before you get upset and call PETA, think about it—there are worse ways to go.

MIXOLOGY

1 can of Milwaukee's Best

Empty jar of salsa

Open that can of Beast and pour it into your salsa jar until it is a third full. Bury the jar in your garden, with the lip of the jar level with the ground.

---

② THE DRINK THAT WILL IMPRESS . . .

> *"Why don't you get out of that wet coat and into a dry Martini?"*—Robert Benchley

Like your clothes, shoes, and facial piercings, a cocktail says many things about you. It might say: Wow, this guy ordered six cocktail onions in his drink. Now here's someone who knows exactly what he wants. Or it might say: Six cocktail onions? One drink? What, is he making a stew?

Or it could possibly say: There's no way I'm kissing someone who can eat a half-dozen of those salty little suckers without flinching. It all depends on who your cocktail is addressing. Consider what your drink is saying to . . .

the Babe Sitting on the Barstool Next to You

 RED WINE

"A glass of red shows that the guy is romantic, classy, and intelligent," was the consensus of an informal poll of a dozen women. I admit, this wasn't the most scientific poll in the world, but did you ever try to get 12 women to agree about anything?

TIPS FROM THE CELLAR

Want to fool someone into thinking you actually purchase and sip fine wine all of the time? Here's a cheater's guide to popular wines and their pronunciations:

1.	Cabernet Sauvignon	CAB-er-NAY saw vee NYON
2.	Pinot Noir	PEE-noh NWAHR
3.	Merlot	mer-LOH
4.	Chardonnay	shar-dohn-NAY
5.	Thunderbird	thun-duh-BOID

DRINKS TO AVOID IN THIS SITUATION: A mug of Budweiser ("He's cheap and clueless"), a Bloody Mary ("Boozy tomato breath—ew!"), or a Margarita. "It's seriously suspect and severely feminine," says one woman of the Mexican favorite. "Ole? Oh, gay!"

MIX IT RIGHT: Want to really impress her? Get specific. "The more specific it is in terms of where the wine comes from," says Richard Vadya, lead instructor at the New York Restaurant School, "the more expensive." In short, if the label says FROM SOMEWHERE IN EUROPE, it's probably cheap. If the label says FROM THE NAPA VALLEY OF CALIFORNIA, STAG'S LEG REGION, FOURTH VINEYARD OVER, ROW C, VINE 43-A, PICKED BY MR. ERNESTO AT 4:45 P.M. DURING A SOLAR ECLIPSE, it's probably expensive. Why do specifics translate into higher quality? "It usually means fully ripened grapes, healthier vines, and a wine that was more carefully made, not to mention heavier and richer," says Vadya. With vaguely labeled bottles, it's more of a crapshoot.

Your Colleagues

 DAIQUIRI

Jennings Cox had a problem. There he was, down in Cuba, expecting a few colleagues for drinks, and he was plum out of gin. All Cox had was the native spirit, rum. He couldn't serve rum to civilized people, could he? Then the bright mining executive had an idea. He would mix in lime juice and sugar and hopefully mask the rum enough to make it a worthy cocktail. Thus was born the Daiquiri—supposedly. Of course, Cubans were probably enjoying these sweet-yet-sharp cocktails long before Jennings Cox had his gringo butt assigned to the country. Since that day in 1896, the Daiquiri has gone on to score many important admirers, among them Ernest Hemingway, F. Scott Fitzgerald—even J.F.K. It should impress the boys in accounting, don't you think?

MIXOLOGY

1¹/2 oz. light rum

³/4 oz. lime juice

¹/4 oz. simple syrup

Lime wedge or wheel

Shake rum, lime, and syrup with cracked ice, then strain into a chilled cocktail glass. Garnish with lime.

Your Lawyer

 BACARDI COCKTAIL

In 1936, the Bacardi Company sued a bunch of New York bars that were supposedly serving "Bacardi Cocktails" but using cheap rail rum instead of the real deal. Bacardi triumphed; the rum police will come after you if you mix this drink using a different brand. Buy your lawyer another one if he picks up his cell phone and starts calling the Captain Morgan people.

MIXOLOGY

11/2 oz. Bacardi rum—and only Bacardi rum, wiseguy.

1 oz. lime juice

1 tsp. grenadine

Maraschino cherry

Pour the Bacardi, lime juice, and grenadine in a shaker full of ice. Shake, then strain into a cocktail glass. Top with cherry.

Your Grandmother

 SIDECAR

This 1920s-era cocktail is enjoying a renaissance in swank New York watering holes like Angel's Share in the East Village and the Red Cat in Chelsea, according to the *New York Times*. "Most people these days ordering sidecars have been turned on to them," said Connor Coffey, a bartender at the Red Cat. "It's not a drink they've seen on *Sex and the City*." The sidecar's origins are a bit murky; two Parisian bars lay claim to

the invention. Popular cocktail legend has it that a World War I officer hopped out of his chauffeur-driven sidecar and demanded something to warm him up, so a bartender at a.) the Ritz's Little Bar or b.) Harry's New York Bar whipped up this trifecta. Who was it? Who cares! This is a cocktail worth rediscovering, even if you travel in a vehicle with a roof on it.

MIXOLOGY

1 1/2 oz. brandy

3/4 oz. Cointreau

3/4 oz. freshly squeezed
lemon juice

Pour everything into a shaker filled with ice. Shake the hell out of it—as if you're riding in the sidecar of a Harley Davidson— then strain into a chilled cocktail glass.

MIX IT RIGHT: Fresh lemon juice is key; use lemonade or artificial lemon juice and the Sidecar runs the risk of tasting too sweet. One sign if you're in a bar where they know what they're doing: the bartender will ask you if you want the rim of your glass dusted with confectioners' sugar, or left alone. (It's up to you. If you're the kind of person who digs a salt rim on a Margarita, go for it.)

Your Ultra-Conservative Right-Wing Grandfather

 OLD FASHIONED

Invented circa 1900 by Colonel James Pepper, a whiskey distiller in Louisville, but popularized by Cole Porter in his song, "Make It Another Old Fashioned, Please." The OF became so popular they named the glass after it. If your grandfather wasn't drinking one of these back in the day, he just wasn't drinking at all.

MIXOLOGY

1 1/2 oz. bourbon   Lemon twist

2 dashes Angostura bitters   Pineapple slice

Club soda   Maraschino cherry

Sugar cube

Place the sugar cube in the bottom of a—get this—old fashioned glass and soak it with the bitters. Pour in enough club soda to cover the sugar, then muddle the living hell out of it. Add ice, bourbon, and all that damn fruit. Don't stir! Top with club soda.

Your Other Grandfather, the Pervert

 ANGEL'S TIT

This naughty, ultra-sweet cocktail was a big hit during Prohibition. What makes it naughty? Er, well, uh, there's that matter of the bountiful puff of cream on top of the drink, accented by a bright red cherry in the middle. Still don't get it? Well, you see, the female breast is shaped much like— ah, go ask your camp counselor.

MIXOLOGY

1 1/2 oz. Maraschino liqueur

3/4 oz. cream

Maraschino cherry

Pour the liqueur into a cocktail glass, float a big puff of cream on top (depending on the angel's cup size, of course), then strategically place the cherry in the center.

MIX IT RIGHT: Maraschino liqueur—like angels—can be tough to find in this less-than-innocent world; substitute crème de cacao (and skip the cherry) and you've got an Angel's Tip. Naked Barbie dolls have Angel's Tips.

a Female Date, When You Order It for Her

 VANIL AND GINGER

Of course, you should ask your ladyfriend if she has a preference first. Maybe she's a white wine gal, or a Cosmo sipper, or even a Kentucky bourbon slugger. But if she looks to you for a recommendation, give this a try. This sweet-yet-potentially-serious drink has a lot going for it. Vanil and Ginger is a relatively new cocktail, so she won't associate it (and you) with bad college parties; it's vanilla-sweet enough to slip past her tongue easily, yet strong enough for her to feel the warmth of the vodka slipping down her throat. Sweet and warm. Those are two good associations, no?

MIXOLOGY

1 oz. Stoli Vanil

3 oz. ginger ale

Gently mix both ingredients in a mixing glass, then serve in a chilled rocks glass over ice.

MIX IT RIGHT: Freezer ice has the amazing ability to mimic the odor and tastes of the objects that surround it. Unfortunately, that means your cocktail ice probably tastes like frozen pizza, Hungry-Man fried chicken, and a tin foil-wrapped lump that is suspiciously marked W. DISNEY 12/15/66. Instead, buy a bag of cocktail-sized ice cubes from the supermarket and scoop 'em out fresh from the bag (or an ice bucket). If you're stuck with your freezer cubes, try rinsing them in cold tap water; this should remove freezer burn and eau de Walt.

a Male Date, When You Order It for Him

 ## WHATEVER YOU'RE HAVING

Of course, you should ask your guy if he has a preference first. Maybe he's a gin and tonic kind of guy, or a Scotch sipper, or even a Piña Colada chugger. (If it's the latter, run.) But if he looks to you for a recommendation, give him whatever you're having. "If a man and a woman are on a date, the man will go with what the woman is drinking," said Liz Wayne, owner of Manhattan bar SX137, in the *New York Times.* "That's the trend." Of course, this is an updated version of a classic dating move: mirroring. Oh, you enjoy carving ice statues with a chainsaw, too? What a coincidence! So, in an effort to appear less frat-boy, the man will want to impress you with his tolerance of so-called "chick drinks"—cocktails with a lot of fruit, or flavored vodka, or both.

MIXOLOGY

Some trendy "chick drinks" in this book include:

Retro Hipster Friends

PEGU CLUB COCKTAIL

This forgotten favorite was invented at the Pegu Club near Rangoon during the 1930s, and it became wildly popular within ten years. It is made with readily available ingredients, and it is awaiting rediscovery. Go for it, hepcat.

MIXOLOGY

1 1/2 oz. gin	1 dash orange bitters
3/4 oz. curacao	1 dash lime juice
1 dash Angostura bitters	

Put everything into a mixing glass full of ice. Stir for a bit, then strain into a chilled cocktail glass.

British Royalty

 HIS ROYAL HIGHNESS

According to the 1934 mixology tome *My New Cocktail Book*: "The below recipe was given to the Ritz-Carlton Hotel in Montreal, by his Royal Highness [the Prince of Wales], with instructions that this was the cocktail that he wanted served to him at all times." It's good to be the prince.

MIXOLOGY

1/8 part Italian vermouth

1/8 part French vermouth

1/8 part orange curacao

1/8 part sugar syrup

1/4 part dry gin

1/4 part brandy

Mix everything in an ice-filled highball glass.

---

a Con Artist

 AMERICANO

During Prohibition, expatriates in need of a stiff one fled to Europe, and in Italy some clever wags discovered Campari, which technically qualified as bitters. And bitters could be legally brought to the United States, because they were deemed "medicinal" products. To honor American ingenuity—or, rather, sneakiness—this cocktail was dubbed "the Americano." And we wonder why the rest of the world doesn't trust us?

MIXOLOGY

1 oz. Campari

1/2 oz. sweet vermouth

Club soda

Orange slice

Stir the Campari and sweet vermouth in a highball glass filled with ice, then add club soda to fill and garnish with the orange.

MIX IT RIGHT: Americanos were too wimpy for Count Camillo Negroni, an aristocrat from Florence who barhopped more than frat boys on St. Paddy's Day. Negroni insisted that gin be added instead of the club soda, and the result, of course, was the Negroni: 1 oz. Campari, 1 oz. sweet vermouth, and 2 oz. gin. Same mixing instructions as above, more of a kick in the pants.

Julia Roberts

 SCORPINO

This Portuguese cocktail is a favorite of Ms. Roberts—at least it was when she appeared on *Oprah* a short while back. Then again, it might have staying power. Reportedly, Ms. Roberts's dog is named "Scorpino."

MIXOLOGY

2 oz. vodka

1 oz. Cointreau

2 oz. cream

1 scoop lemon Italian ice

Put everything into a blender, then serve in a Champagne flute.

MIX IT RIGHT: When using a blender, don't overdo it. You're blending drink ingredients, not trying to split every last atom. A couple of rotations of the swirling blades should be enough.

the Morton's Seafood Guy

 OYSTER SHOOTER

And you thought Rocky swallowing a glass of raw eggs was disgusting? This literal seafood cocktail is not for chickens of the sea. It was invented by Manhattan's Live Bait, as reported by *Details* magazine.

MIXOLOGY

Raw oyster in its juice	1 shot Absolut Peppar vodka
1 dash Tabasco sauce	Lemon wedge
1 dash cocktail sauce	Ground black pepper

Combine the first four ingredients in a tumbler. Add a squeeze of lemon, and dash the freshly ground pepper on top.

MIX IT RIGHT: "Most bartenders get sloppy with recipes," grouses Buddy Dorton, a 20-year vet bartender at Hank's Seafood in Charleston, South Carolina. "They don't care if they've got too much of one ingredient or not enough of another. They don't shake a cocktail well, either. And if a recipe calls for a squeeze of lemon, it needs a squeeze of lemon. How hard is that? It's just a squeeze of lemon."

the Editors of *The Guinness Book of World Records*

 BIG RITA

If you want to earn the title of "World's Largest Cocktail" in the *Guinness Book of World Records*, you're going to have to do better than Big Rita, which won the honor during the First Annual Phloridays Parrothead Phestival in Orlando, Florida, in May 2001. Our tip: Stick with something easy, like a Screwdriver.

MIXOLOGY

5,250 gallons Margarita mix

1,313 gallons tequila

437 gallons Rose's triple sec

Combine in a 7,500 gallon FDA-approved polyethylene tank.

Blend with an upside-down helicopter.

 MIX IT RIGHT: For a single serving, just mix 1 oz. tequila, 1/2 oz. triple sec, and the juice of half a lime in a glass with cracked ice.

③ THE DRINK FOR MAJOR LIFE EVENTS

> *"I can't die until the government finds a safe place to bury my liver."*—Phil Harris

Shakespeare described the seven stages of man as infant, school-boy, lover, soldier, justice, elder statesman, and finally old age, in which man is "sans teeth, sans eyes, sans taste, sans everything." But Willie Shakes missed quite a few stages. And for each of these stages, there is the perfect drink to guide you through it. (Shakes didn't think of these, either. Somebody want to tell me why everyone thinks Shakespeare is such a big deal?)

First Holy Communion/ Bar or Bat Mitzvah

 SHIRLEY TEMPLE

After the rigors of this coming-of-age ritual, you need a good stiff one. Problem is, adults tend to be touchy about kids knocking back with a bottle. (Like they were never in grade school before? Sheesh!) The next best thing is this age-old age-be-damned classic. If you're in grade school right now and reading this book, you probably have no freakin' idea who Shirley Temple was. Ignorance is bliss, kid. Stir shallow and drink deep. You've got quite a few years before your next cocktail.

MIXOLOGY

Ginger ale   Maraschino cherries

3 dashes grenadine   Miniature plastic sword

Pour the ginger ale into a glass filled with ice, add the grenadine, and then stir. Include a couple maraschino cherries. Pierce the cherries with a miniature plastic sword. Kids dig that kind of thing.

First Frat Party

 JUNGLE JUICE

There's only one time in your life where you can get away with drinking the foulest, fruitiest drink on Earth out of a trash receptacle, and brother, this is that time.

MIXOLOGY

1 bottle Everclear

An absurd amount of Hawaiian Punch Fruit Juicy Red

6 oranges (if you're feeling fancy)

Take a relatively clean trashcan and line with plastic. Pour the ingredients, mix to taste, and start calling the babes.

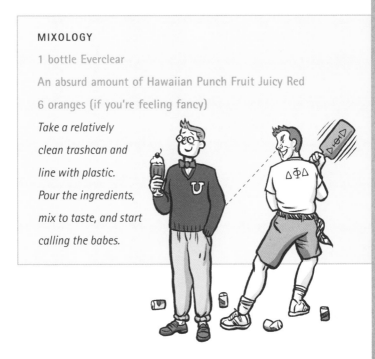

MIX IT RIGHT: Andrea Immer, *Esquire's* wine writer, came up with a classier version of Jungle Juice, in case you ever want to relive your college days without having to drink something out of a trash can. Her recipe calls for 1 oz. Everclear, 1 oz. Captain Morgan, 3/4 oz. peach nectar, 1/2 oz. apricot brandy, 2 oz. pineapple juice, and 2 oz. cranberry juice. Pour everything into a shaker filled with ice, then strain into an ice-filled pint glass. (Use one with your alma mater's logo, if it'll make you feel special. Or one of those dirty white plastic cups they used to hand out at frat keggers.) Garnish with a pineapple wedge or maraschino cherry.

THE DRINK TO AVOID IN THIS SITUATION: When you're in college, anything goes. But remember the golden rule: beer before liquor, never sicker. Liquor before beer, never fear. In other words: if you plan to rumble in the jungle all night, pass up those early-evening cans of Milwaukee's Best.

While Under the Age of 21

 GIN GIMLET

No underage drinker in his/her right mind would order a Gin Gimlet, and bartenders know this. Of course, there's a reason no underage drinkers order it—to the young, untrained tongue, a Gimlet tastes like Sprite and gasoline. But those are the breaks, kid. You could either be in a swank nightclub or out with your buddies on the street corner passing a 40-ouncer back and forth. Your call.

MIXOLOGY

1¹/2 oz. gin

1/2 oz. lime juice

Shake with ice and strain into a cocktail glass.

THE DRINK TO AVOID IN THIS SITUATION: Anything with "sex" in its name (e.g., "Sex on the Beach," "Sex on the Bartop," "Sex with My New Prison Friends").

Your 21st Birthday

 KAMIKAZE

This is one of the last times it'll be acceptable to order a drink like this in mixed company (the other is your bachelor/bachelorette party), so enjoy it now.

MIXOLOGY

1 oz. vodka

1 oz. triple sec

1 oz. lime juice

Pour into an ice-filled shaker and round up two other suckers. Shake and strain into three shot glasses.

THE DRINK TO AVOID IN THIS SITUATION: The free cup of coffee they give you in the drunk tank the following morning.

Your Best Buddy's 21st Birthday and You Still Haven't Forgiven Him for the Time He Put "Icy-Hot" in Your Jock Strap

 BUFFALO SWEAT

Even an entire battalion of Kamikazes won't banish the memory of this hardboiled rite of passage. Just make sure you've already had your twenty-first birthday before trying this on someone else.

MIXOLOGY

1 oz. bourbon

3 dashes Tabasco sauce

Dump into a shot glass, then take a rag and wipe up the bartop—maybe clean the jukebox and framed mirrors while you're at it—then wring it into the shot glass.

While Saving Yourself for Marriage

SLOE SCREWS

Want to preserve your virginity? Simply order any one of these fine high-balls at your local watering hole. Order loudly, so people can hear you. There's absolutely no chance you'll get lucky.

Sloe Screw

MIXOLOGY

1 1/2 oz. vodka

1 oz. sloe gin

Orange juice to fill

Mix everything in an ice-filled highball glass.

Sloe Comfortable Screw

MIXOLOGY

1 1/2 oz. vodka

1 oz. sloe gin

1 oz. Southern Comfort

Orange juice to fill

Mix everything in an ice-filled highball glass.

Sloe Comfortable Screw up Against the Wall

MIXOLOGY

1 1/2 oz. vodka

1 oz. sloe gin

1 oz. Southern Comfort

Orange juice to fill

1 oz. Galliano

Mix the first four ingredients in an ice-filled highball glass,
then float the Galliano on top.

Your First Real Job

 URINE SAMPLE

Better this yellow drink than smoking up a bushel of fifth generation, hydroponically-grown Hawaiian Gold the night before your first day on the job.

MIXOLOGY

1/2 oz. Galliano

1/2 oz. Midori

1/2 oz. vodka

Pour over ice, strain into shot glass.

Marriage

 CHAPEL OF LOVE

This punch, from *Atomic Cocktails*, is the perfect wedding libation, since this is one of the few socially acceptable ways to "share the love" with all of your guests. Unless you come from one of those really kinky families.

MIXOLOGY

750 ml. bottle of chilled white Rioja wine

750 ml. bottle of chilled medium-sweet Reisling wine

750 ml. bottle chilled Moscato wine

3/4 cup orange juice

3/4 cup grapefruit juice

11 oz. bottle Orange Perrier, chilled

8 strawberries

2 starfruit, sliced

2 kiwi fruit, sliced

Pour everything except the fruit into a large punch bowl, then refrigerate for one hour. Pull it out after you say your "I Do's," and float the strawberries, starfruit, and kiwi on top.

First-Time Father

 DIRTY DIAPER

You might imagine yourself sipping at a flute of Champagne while the scent of congratulatory cigar smoke fills the air of the gentlemen's club as your friends and colleagues toast your ability to contribute the genetic material necessary to bring a new life into this world—but who are you kidding? Brace yourself with this shot and get ready for the real thing.

MIXOLOGY

3/4 oz. vodka

3/4 oz. Amaretto

3/4 oz. Southern Comfort

3/4 oz. Midori

3/4 oz. Chambord

3/4 oz. orange juice

Pour over ice, then strain into four shot glasses. Find three other dads.

First-Time Mother

BROWN COW FROM HELL

This drink is refreshing and innocent, yet reminds you of what you feel like if you're nursing the kid every two hours: a friggin' cow. "It's disturbing that I'm not 'Mommy,' but just another food group," opined one new mother. Don't worry about the Kahlua—it'll knock the kid out just enough so that you can give your udders a break for a couple of hours. (Caveat: Most doctors will say that a small alcoholic beverage now and again is completely fine, but check with your own physician first.)

MIXOLOGY

2 oz. Kahlua

Cold milk

Chocolate syrup to taste

Pour everything into a highball glass and stir until there's no syrup left at the bottom of the glass.

Divorce

THE ANTICHRIST

Might as well get up close and personal with the person to whom you're going to have to sell your soul in order to keep your home, car, checking account, golf clubs, stereo, self-esteem . . .

MIXOLOGY

1/2 oz. Everclear

1/2 oz. Bacardi rum

1/2 oz. Absolut Peppar

3 dashes Tabasco sauce

Mix all liquors in a shot glass, then add the Tabasco on top.

MIX IT RIGHT: For most mixed drinks, use light or gold rum. Save the dark stuff for sipping.

Second Marriage

WALLIS COCKTAIL

In 1936 the Duke of Windsor served this preprandial delight to celebrate his wedding. But it was a bittersweet affair; months earlier, the Duke—then Edward VIII, King of England—had chosen to marry two-time American divorcée Wallis Simpson. The Church of England had a big problem with divorce, Parliament refused to bestow a title on Simpson, and the English people were horrified that their king would shack up with a Yank divorcée. Rather than throw his country into chaos, Edward VIII gave up the crown and became the Duke of Windsor. Tell this story to anyone who doesn't think that second marriages are romantic.

MIXOLOGY

1¹/₂ oz. Cointreau	3 oz. gin
1¹/₂ oz. peppermint	³/₄ oz. lemon juice
schnapps	Soda water

Pour everything except the soda water into an ice-filled shaker, shake, and strain into a cocktail glass with ice, then fill the rest of the way with soda water.

Third Marriage and Up

 A KEG OF BEER

Let's face it: you're not going to be getting hitched again in a church or synagogue. You'll probably have it in somebody's backyard. Maybe even your own. Do you really want to deal with Champagne, mixed drinks, or wine? No way. If you set the expectation bar low, you might find yourself pleasantly surprised. That goes for the beer, too. In the words of Terry Lennox from Raymond Chandler's *The Long Goodbye*: "Alcohol is like love. The first kiss is magic, the second is intimate, the third routine. After that you take the girl's clothes off."

MIXOLOGY

1 Keg of beer   Plastic cups

1 Tap

1. *Let the keg settle for 1/2 hour after you bring it home.*

2. *Clean off the tap area with a clean, wet rag—if you don't, the seal won't be tight, and that means foam.*

3. *Put the tap on the top of the keg and turn until it locks down in the notches. Turn it hard, so it's nice and flat against the lip. Everything should be locked in.*

---

4. Push the little metal stub at the bottom of the tap to release pressure inside and reduce foam.

5. Pour your first three beers by aiming the black plastic tap head down into a cup. These will be foamy; it's normal. After the fourth beer, the foam factor should go way down. If it doesn't, you probably don't have a tight seal. Unlock it and try again.

6. Pump the keg when the stream of heavenly suds slows up. Pour while pumping, so you know when the beer is flowing again.

MIX IT RIGHT: Not sure how much beer you're going to need to slake the thirsty wedding hordes? Consult this handy chart.

TYPE OF CONTAINER	GALLONS	CASES	INDIVIDUAL BEERS
Case	2.5	1	24
Beer ball	5.2	2.33	56
Pony keg	7.75	3.44	83
Keg	15.5	6.89	165
Barrel	31	13.78	331
Truckload	5,000	2,000	48,000
Rail car load	180,000	7,200	172,800

You've Hit a Wall in Your Career

 HARVEY WALLBANGER

Pretty much a Screwdriver with a couple of dashes of Galliano—and surprise, surprise! The makers of Galliano put forth a huge "Harvey Wallbanger" ad campaign in the 1970s, featuring a cartoon character named "Harvey." However, if the drink's creation story is to be believed, the drink is named for a manic-depressive surfer who wiped out, then proceeded to smash his head against a wall until he could be calmed down with liquor. (One wonders why Disney hasn't picked this up for feature-length treatment.)

MIXOLOGY

1 1/2 oz. vodka

4 oz. orange juice

1/2 oz. Galliano

Pour the vodka and OJ into a chilled collins glass with ice.

Stir well, then top with the Galliano.

Midlife Crisis

 BOILERMAKER

Because sometimes a beer just isn't enough.

> **MIXOLOGY**
>
> Beer
>
> 1½ oz. blended whiskey
>
> *Pour the beer into a mug. Pour the whiskey into the beer.*
> *Repeat as needed.*

MIX IT RIGHT: Want a fancier version? Pour the whiskey into a shot glass first, then drop it into the beer and watch it plunge to the bottom like all of your hopes and dreams. This is called a Depth Charge. Cute, huh? Yeah.

The Marriage of Your Child

 BAIRN

"Bairn" is the Scottish word for "child," and it is an affectionate title. It's pronounced bear-RRRRnnnn and sounds great when you moan it drunkenly with a fake brogue in a corner of a reception hall. Have your significant other explain that it's a "Scottish wedding thing," even if you're African-American.

MIXOLOGY

1 1/2 oz. Scotch

3/4 oz. Cointreau

2 or 3 dashes orange bitters

Pour everything into an ice-filled shaker, shake, then strain into a chilled cocktail glass.

The Birth of Your First Grandchild

 ART LINKLETTER'S PAPAYA COCKTAIL

Because your grandkid will say the darndest things.

MIXOLOGY

2 oz. papaya juice

1 oz. dry sherry

Serve in a cocktail glass.

Retirement

 A VINTAGE WINE

This is the kind of treat you should prepare ahead of time. Buy the wine long before you actually plan to retire, and it'll be there waiting for you when you finally cash in your career chips. You and the wine will have aged together, fermented together, rotted in cellars together. You'll have a lot to talk about. My parents bought me a 1989 Bordeaux for my high school graduation, and I'm comforted by the fact that it'll be there when I finally decide to hang it up and enjoy the good life. Or at least until I run out of other wine and the liquor store is closed for the night.

> **MIXOLOGY**
> *Find a wine from either the year you graduated high school or college, or the first year you started adult employment.*
> *Note: if you're Strom Thurmond, take that year and add 50, just so you'll be able to find something still in existence.*

When Senility Strikes

THE DRINK WITHOUT A NAME

This cocktail, still awaiting a proper name, was created by Paul Harrington, author of *Cocktail* and the official alchemist at www.cocktailtime.com. I like it because there are no pesky names to remember. And if you're senile, it'll be a new drink experience every time you order it!

MIXOLOGY

2 oz. vodka

1/4 oz. Cointreau

1 dash Chartreuse

Orange twist

Stir liquids with cracked ice, then strain into a chilled cocktail glass. Garnish with orange twist.

On Your Deathbed

 MITCH'S CURTAIN CALL

A month after Robert Mitchum died, some of his Hollywood buddies gathered a party and started reminiscing about him. One of them said: "What I heard was, Mitch was on his deathbed. Two in the morning he got up, had a shot of tequila, smoked a cigarette, then went back to bed and died." Even if it's not true, it's sounds like an appropriately hard-boiled way to face the Great Beyond. Why not be half-lit when going into the light?

MIXOLOGY

1 1/2 oz. tequila

1 cigarette

Enjoy each to the fullest, then go back to bed and wait for the Grim Reaper to show up.

THE DRINK TO AVOID IN THIS SITUATION: Anything sweet. The Grim Reaper will bitch-slap you if he even so much as sees a bottle of rum in your bedroom.

4 IF YOU'RE IN THE MOOD . . .

Human beings are creatures of mood. What—you don't believe me? Of course we have freakin' moods—we're flesh and blood, damnit, not brainless automatons who go about their meaningless little lives sipping the same insipid cocktails at the same insipid bars like good little corporate zombies! [Author breaks down, sobbing.] I'm so sorry. I can't believe I went off on a rant like that. It's just been tough, you know? Compiling all of these cocktails and not knowing if anybody is actually going to appreciate them, much less want to mix them. It's so hard. [Author sighs.] Still, you might try these drinks if you're in the mood . . .

for Just One Drink

 THE ZOMBIE

This drink was credited to a guy named Don the Beachcomber, whose South Pacific–themed bars started the 1950s/1960s craze for anything tiki, bamboo, or Polynesian. Don claimed that only one zombie could be served to a customer per night. "Why people drink them I don't know," admitted Don in 1945. "Personally, I think it's too damn strong, but people seem to like it that way."

MIXOLOGY

2 oz. light Puerto Rican rum	1 oz. orange juice
1 oz. dark Jamaican rum	1 oz. pineapple juice
1/2 oz. 151-proof Demerara rum	1/2 oz. papaya or guava juice
1 oz. curacao	1/4 oz. grenadine
1 tsp. Pernod	1/2 oz. sugar syrup
1 oz. lemon juice	Mint sprig
	Pineapple stick

Blend liquids with ice and pour into a chilled glass. Garnish with mint sprig and pineapple stick.

for a Quick Jolt

MATT HELM MARTINI

In Donald Hamilton's 1961 novel *The Removers*, ultra-tough secret agent Matt Helm faces the man who's married his ex-wife. "Are you a Martini or a bourbon man, Mr. Helm?" the new husband asks. Helm replies: "Either one. It depends on the circumstances. For the long haul, bourbon, but for a quick jolt nothing beats a Martini. I think tonight might be classed as a Martini night, Mr. Logan."

MIXOLOGY

3 oz. gin	1 splash Pernod
1 splash dry vermouth	Lemon twist

Shake, then strain into a chilled martini glass. Garnish with lemon twist.

MIX IT RIGHT: Don't dig olives or cocktail onions? There's no rule that says you can't toss in your own garnish to create your own signature Martini. You might try a slice of radish or avocado, or even a small cross-section of dill pickle. Some enjoy three jellybeans. Others, an anchovy. Raw cucumber slices are big with some, as are mushrooms marinated in sweet vermouth.

to Feel Buzzed, but Alert

 ECSTASY IN A CAN

Los Angeles lounge dwellers, tired of feeling woozy after too many Martinis, adopted this Jekyll and Hyde drink. The vodka gives you a nice warm buzz, but the Red Bull will snap your senses to full attention.

This drink has become surprisingly popular in its relatively short life—although Red Bull has been used as a mixer in European bars since the early 1990s. Stockbrokers in London have nicknamed it "Liquid Cocaine," and the *London Times* once warned that "the volatile combination of vodka and Red Bull tastes like alcoholic fruit juice but it gives drinkers such a euphoric high that many are losing control during the traditional Friday night drinking sessions around Bishopsgate." A lot of this is hype—there's nothing in Red Bull that can send you into a frenzy; it's pretty much caffeinated sugar water. And Red Bull alone tastes something like cough medicine, or more charitably, Flintstones chewable vitamins.

MIXOLOGY

1¹/₂ oz. vodka   1 can Red Bull energy drink

Pour the Red Bull into a pint glass, then add the shot of vodka.

---

to Nurse One Drink as Long as You Can

 WHITE RUSSIAN

This is a favorite of Peter Dorelli, head bartender at the prestigious American Bar at the Savoy in London. "It is one of the rare drinks that improves as the ice melts," he writes. "To start with it is rather rich, but it becomes more refreshing."

MIXOLOGY

1 1/2 oz. vodka

3/4 oz. Kahlua

3/4 oz. heavy cream

Fill an old fashioned glass with ice, then add vodka, followed by the Kahlua. Stir gently, like you're negotiating an arms treaty during the Cold War. Add cream on top.

MIX IT RIGHT: Want to make a Black Russian? Just leave out the heavy cream.

93

for Another Cocktail, but You Really Should Have a Coffee

 ESPRESSO MARTINI

"It has to be dark chocolate—that's the secret," explains drink inventor Mark Stevens, bartender at the Federalist in Boston. "And make it good vodka, please."

MIXOLOGY

1 1/2 oz. vodka

1/4 oz. Frangelica

1/4 oz. Bailey's Irish Cream

1/4 oz. Tia Maria

1/4 oz. Godiva Dark Chocolate Liqueur

1/4 oz. hot espresso

Add vodka and liqueurs to shaker with ice, add espresso, and stir briskly. Strain into a martini glass.

MIX IT RIGHT: If you're mixing booze and coffee, pour in the booze first then add the coffee—it will blend more smoothly.

to Erase the Memory of Your Own Name

 BRANDY ALEXANDER
(A.K.A. "MILK SHAKE")

When Lennon temporarily separated from Yoko Ono in 1974 to begin his year-long "Lost Weekend" in L.A., he and Harry Nilsson drank nothing but Brandy Alexanders. (Okay, maybe they consumed other substances, but for more on that you'll have to consult the sequel to this book, *The Perfect Hard Drug for Every Occasion*.) One night the pair became so wildly drunk on Brandy Alexanders, they started heckling the Smothers Brothers at the Troubadour Club and were unceremoniously kicked out. As Buddha Records exec Curtis Armstrong put it, "Harry Nilsson was about to go down in history as the guy who got John Lennon so drunk he forgot himself."

MIXOLOGY

1½ oz. brandy or Cognac   Sweet or ice cream

½ oz. dark crème de cacao

Shake with ice and strain. (Alternate recipe, courtesy of John Lennon: "It's brandy and milk, folks.")

---

to Erase the Memory of Your Own Name, but Not Suffer the Next Morning

 SAKETINI

Sake, Japan's top tipple, exists in a kind of libation Twilight Zone. It's brewed from rice, which makes it closer to beer than any spirit. But sake is not carbonated like beer, and it's much stronger—about 15 to 20 percent alcohol. The best part, however, is that it's an extremely pure beverage that lacks congeners—the impurities in booze that make you want to saw off your head and mail it to Guatemala the next morning.

MIXOLOGY

2 oz. good quality sake

5 oz. vodka

Cucumber slice

Pour the sake and vodka into an ice-filled shaker. Shake, then strain into a martini glass. Garnish with cucumber.

MIX IT RIGHT: You may have noticed that some sushi restaurants serve sake heated. This is because they use cheap sake that needs to be heated to mask the harsh flavor. However, even this doesn't work, since heated sake tastes a lot like Vicks Vapo-Rub. Sake should be served and enjoyed ice cold. Try Gekkeikan, Hakusan, or Kunshu, three of the most popular sakes on the market. (A good bottle will set you back $20.)

for a Girlie Drink with a Manly Name

 MANDATORY

The name conjures images of strict militaristic obedience—do or die, to hell with the danger or consequences. Even the first syllable—MAN—is undeniably masculine. But actually, this drink is about as manly as Nathan Lane. It's sweet and petite. Your grandmother's poodle would love it.

MIXOLOGY

1 oz. Bailey's Irish Cream

1 oz. DeKuyper peppermint schnapps

1 oz. heavy cream

Pour ingredients into an ice-filled shaker, then strain into a small cocktail glass.

---

for a Manly Drink with a Girlie Name

 PINK GIN

It's the word "pink" that throws the whole thing off. You imagine a cloying, sickly sweet concoction like a Daiquiri; what you get is a gin-soaked punch in the mouth. This drink, in fact, is damn close to an ultra-dry Martini or Gibson; only the bitters and fruit garnish separate it from the rest of the rat pack. Leave it to the Brits, who invented this tough-as-nails drink, to give it a squishy name—based on the fact that the orangey Angostura bitters gives the gin a pink hue. Fine. You can't mess with chemistry. But couldn't they have named it "Pink Armageddon," or something?

MIXOLOGY

3 oz. gin   Lemon or lime twist

2 dashes Angostura bitters

Shake with ice, strain into a chilled martini glass. Garnish with a twist of lemon or lime.

to Play—and Win—a Drinking Game

 FAKE AND TONIC

This drink will pass the essential sniff test and maybe even the sip test, since the tonic water will fool even the most discerning taste buds. Only you'll know the difference. (And only you will remember what the hell happened that night.)

MIXOLOGY

6 oz. tonic water   Lime wedge

1 splash gin or vodka

With your back to the rest of the partygoers, combine the two ingredients in a highball glass with loads of ice, adding as little booze as humanly possible. Garnish with lime.

MIX IT RIGHT: Tonic water is carbonated sugar water with lemon and quinine, and it tastes bitter. Soda water is just carbonated water, without any flavor either way. You know that liter bottle of tonic water you bought to mix up a few G&Ts? It's going to go flat after one night. If you're mixing drinks for a smaller party—you and your two cats—you're better off picking up a bunch of 12-ounce bottles.

to Blow $10,800 on a Round of Drinks

SPRINGBANK 1919 MALT WHISKEY

At $10,800 a bottle, it's one of the most expensive bottles of hooch on Earth. Of course, if you consider ten grand merely chump change, you should have a rare wine dealer scare up a bottle of Chateau d'Yquem Sauternes (1787), which goes for $56,000 to $64,000 per bottle according to *The Guinness Book of World Records*. Thomas Jefferson was supposed to have loved the stuff and even introduced it to his drinking buddy, George Washington.

MIXOLOGY

Springbank 1919 Malt Whiskey

Rocks glass

$100 bills

Cigar

Pour the Springbank into the rocks glass. Ignite one of the $100 bills and use it to light your cigar. Sip at the whiskey. Repeat as needed, or until your manservants carry you off to bed.

---

to Drink

 PROHIBITION COCKTAIL

"For the benefit of those who are driving, or who may be bluenosed, on the wagon, strongly principled, or under doctor's orders," writes Ted Shane in his 1950 paperback *Bar Guide*. All fine reasons, but Mr. Shane forgot the best of all: you just don't feel like having any booze. There comes a time in every adult's life when it is simply time to Just Say Whoah. This fruity, fizzy concoction is complex enough to keep it interesting anyway.

MIXOLOGY

3 oz. grape juice	Raspberry syrup to taste
1 1/2 oz. lemon juice	Ginger ale
1 oz. lime juice	Mint sprig

Mix all of the fruity stuff first, then pour over ice cubes in a tall glass, fill with ginger ale, and add the mint.

---

⑤ THE PERFECT HOLIDAY LIBATION

Holidays were invented for two reasons: To pause from the daily grind and to gather with relatives to renew the bonds of familial love. And to drink enough booze to get you through the trauma of gathering with relatives and renewing the bonds of familial love. Whether you're celebrating an important religious event or just another Hallmark holiday, here is the perfect drink for . . .

New Year's Day

 MIMOSA

You wake up New Year's Day. What do you have, aside from invisible elves using tiny ball peen hammers on the inside of your skull and the general ennui that precedes another year of struggle and unfulfilled destiny? Why, leftover Champagne! Take the dead Moët out of the fridge and whip up this eye-opening classic to go along with your dry toast. This cocktail was introduced in 1925 by the Ritz Hotel in Paris and named after the tropical flowering shrub of the same name—just the thing to put the color back in your cheeks.

MIXOLOGY

3 oz. orange juice

2 dashes Grand Marnier

Champagne

Take a Champagne flute—if you have any still clean from last night—and pour in orange juice and Grand Marnier, then fill the rest of the way with the bubbly.

January 25th

ROB ROY

Today we toast the birth of Robert Burns, the Scottish poet, who gave the world the immortal verse, "When chapman billies leave the street / and drouthy neebors neebors meet. . . ." Oh, who am I kidding? It's late January, we've got the post-holiday blues and we need a nice, classic stiff cocktail. Any holiday'll do.

> 1 1/2 oz. Scotch
> 3/4 oz. sweet vermouth
> 2 dashes Angostura bitters
> Maraschino cherry
>
> *Pour the Scotch and vermouth into a mixing glass full of ice.*
> *Add the bitters, stir three times, then strain into a chilled*
> *cocktail glass. Garnish with a cherry.*

MIX IT RIGHT: Never use single-malt Scotch as a mixer in a cock-tail—it's like using Dom Perignon to douse a campfire.

Presidents' Day

 WASHINGTON COCKTAIL

I cannot tell a lie: if you really want to hoist one in honor of George Washington, have a nice porter, which Washington brewed at Mount Vernon. But this tasty, official-sounding drink will do just fine, too.

MIXOLOGY

2 oz. dry vermouth

1 oz. brandy

1 tsp. fine sugar

1 dash Angostura bitters

Pour everything into an ice-filled shaker, shake well, then strain into a chilled cocktail glass.

Valentine's Day (for Gals)

 CHOCOLATE MARTINI

This cocktail is sweet and about as neat as a felt-covered heart wrapped up in a ribbon. He'll be impressed you ordered a Martini; you'll be grateful it doesn't taste like gasoline.

MIXOLOGY

2 oz. vodka

1/2 oz. crème de cacao

Pour both into an ice-filled shaker, shake, and strain into a chilled martini glass.

Valentine's Day (for Guys)

GENTLEMAN JACK'S SOUR APPLE KISS

This drink was recommended by the fine folks at Jack Daniel's in Lynchburg, Tennessee. The rationale? The tangy, tart smack of this drink will make even the toughest guy want to pucker up.

MIXOLOGY

1/2 oz. Gentleman Jack Rare Tennessee Whiskey

1/2 oz. sour mix

1/2 oz. apple schnapps

Green apple slice

Combine all liquids in a shaker with ice. Shake and strain into a chilled cocktail glass. Garnish with a slice of green apple.

Valentine's Day (for People Who Hate Valentine's Day)

 RED DEATH

The grenadine imparts that deep, dark, arterial ketchup color that makes this drink pleasing to the eye, so don't be stingy with it. It also tastes as nasty and bitter as you feel.

> **MIXOLOGY**
>
> 1/2 oz. vodka   1/2 oz. triple sec
>
> 1/2 oz. sloe gin   1/2 oz. lime juice
>
> 1/2 oz. Southern Comfort   1/2 oz. orange juice
>
> 1/2 oz. Amaretto   1 splash grenadine
>
> *Pour everything except the grenadine into a highball glass*
> *filled with ice. Then splash in the grenadine like blood from a*
> *pierced heart. Stir three times.*

Leap Year

LEAP YEAR

If the *Savoy Cocktail Book* is correct, this drink was concocted by Harry Craddock at the Savoy Hotel in London in time for the 1928 Leap Year party—which would make this drink barely 20 years old.

MIXOLOGY

2 oz. gin

1/2 oz. sweet vermouth

1/2 oz. Grand Marnier

1/4 oz. lemon juice

Lemon or orange twist

Shake with cracked ice, strain into a chilled cocktail glass, and garnish with a twist of lemon or orange.

MIX IT RIGHT: "Learn to cut garnishes," advises Scott Young, president of Extremebartending.com. "Cocktails are all about presentation, the little extras."

Purim

PURIM PUNCH

Of all the Jewish holidays, Purim is the most festive—in fact, on this day good Jews are encouraged to drink heavily. "To be honest, though," explains one Jewish friend, "all of our holidays can be summed up as follows: Someone tried to kill us, we survived, let's drink." The recipe below is essentially Sangria punch, but with a few Judaic grace notes: a bottle of Manischewitz in place of the typical red wine, and 2 cups of Doc Brown's Cel-Ray soda—that's celery soda to you *goyim*.

MIXOLOGY

3 apples	2 tbs. Cognac
2 oranges	10 ice cubes
1 cup orange juice	2 cups Doc Brown's
1 bottle Manischewitz	Cel-Ray soda

Peel the apples and dice them into small cubes. Ditto for the oranges. Mix everything—except the ice and soda—in a large punch bowl. Add the ice and Doc Brown's right before serving.

St. Patrick's Day

 A PINT OF GUINNESS

Shockingly, British drink giant Diageo, the makers of Guinness, have been developing a speedier method of dispensing pints. The new technique uses ultrasonic waves to produce the trademark foamy head instantly, and it has Guinness lovers in Ireland utterly horrified. "If you pull a pint for an Irishman in less than a minute, he'll ask you where the hell you drug that from," one Dublin pub owner told a CNN reporter.

MIXOLOGY

Take a clean, dry 20-ounce pint glass and hold it under the Guinness spigot at a 45-degree angle. Turn on the spigot until the pint glass is 3/4 full. Allow the pint to completely settle— this can take anywhere from one to two minutes—until you top it off. Now take a bar spoon and draw a shamrock in the foam—or use a plastic shamrock cut-out.

THE DRINK TO AVOID IN THIS SITUATION: Green beer. Like its ham and egg counterparts, green beer is better left to children's fantasy books.

Easter

 RAMOS FIZZ

If you feel like you've been dead for three days and need a Sunday morning pick-me-up, roll the tombstone aside and find yourself an egg to make this tasty variation of the New Orleans Gin Fizz.

MIXOLOGY

2 oz. gin	Several dashes orange-
1/2 oz. lime juice	flower water
1/2 oz. lemon juice	1 egg white
1 tsp. sugar	Club soda
1 tsp. heavy cream	

Mix everything except the club soda in a shaker with cracked ice and pour into a collins glass—or even a pilsner. Fill with cold club soda and stir. (According to some recipes, you can even use a blender to combine the ingredients, again adding the soda last.)

MIX IT RIGHT: Orange-flower water is a distillation of bitter orange blossoms, used in both mixed drinks and baked goods.

April 15th

 WEEP NO MORE

Right after you sign on the dotted line and fold up your 1040EZ, mix up this cocktail from drinks writer Kathy Hamlin to take your mind off the pain. If you can't quite wrap your mind around any more numbers tonight, two fifths of Jack Daniel's will do just as nicely.

MIXOLOGY

1½ oz. Cognac   1 splash lime juice

1½ oz. Dubonnet   1 dash Maraschino liqueur

Blend with ice, serve in a chilled cocktail glass.

Arbor Day

 LONE TREE COOLER

You build this drink like you plant a tree—from the ground up. Plus, this drink comes just in time for the return of warm weather, if you live in a part of the country that actually has seasons. Consider it a preview of summer, a harbinger of life—and liver—springing anew.

MIXOLOGY:

Club soda

½ tsp. powdered sugar

2 oz. gin

½ oz. dry vermouth

Lemon twist

Orange spiral

Stir the powdered sugar and 2 oz. carbonated water together in a collins glass. Fill with crushed ice, then pour in the gin and vermouth. Add more carbonated water to fill and stir once more. Finally, top with the foliage: a twist of lemon and the orange spiral.

May 5th

 CINCO DE MAYO

Actually, the drink should be called Diez y seis de Septembre, since the date of the actual Mexican Revolution was September 16, 1910. But even people who had four years of high school Spanish can't wrap their lips around that one, so *viva la cinco!*

MIXOLOGY

3 oz. blanco (white) tequila

1¹/₂ oz. grenadine

1¹/₂ oz. Rose's lime juice

Lime twist

Shake well over ice and pour into a margarita glass. Garnish with lime.

July 4th

 AMERICAN FLAG

In case you haven't guessed, you'll be creating a shot that is red, blue, and white from the bottom up. This also works for Bastille Day, if you think about it. Would you rather celebrate the heritage of Italy? Substitute green crème de menthe for the blue curacao, but pour it on the bottom, then layer in the grenadine and the vodka. Ireland? Layer green crème de menthe, Irish cream, and Grand Marnier. Canada or Poland? Layer grenadine and vodka. Estonia or Zimbabwe? Good luck.

MIXOLOGY

1/2 oz. grenadine

1/2 oz. blue curacao

1/2 oz. vodka

Layer in shot glass in exactly that order.

MIX IT RIGHT: Multi-layered cocktails are called pousse-cafés, pronounced poos ka-FAYS. This is French for "push the coffee." (Come to think of it, "Pousse-Café!" would make a nice slogan for Starbucks.) The science behind every pousse-café is simple: "lighter" liquors will sit nicely on top of "heavier" liquors, and generally liquor with more alcohol tends to be lighter. But these principles of science will only take you so far. Try using smaller glasses, which makes layering easier. Also, pour the different liquors along the bottom of a bar spoon or along two straws, both of which should be touching the side of the glass. Go slow. Nobody's going to call you a "pousse" if you take your time.

If you want to play around with your own pousse-café, consult this handy gravity chart, which runs from lightest to heaviest liquors. In fact, imagine this chart as one huge-ass pousse. (But keep in mind that it's easier to layer three or four liquors with very different weights; layering every single one of the liquors below would never work.)

THE BOOZE	THE GRAVITY	THE SHADE
Southern Comfort	0.97	amber
Tap water	1.00	clear
Green Chartreuse	1.01	green
Cointreau	1.04	white
Peach liqueur	1.04	dark amber
Sloe gin	1.04	dark red
Peppermint schnapps	1.04	white
Brandy	1.04	reddish-brown
Midori	1.05	green
Apricot brandy	1.06	amber
Blackberry brandy	1.06	dark red

Campari	1.06	red
Yellow Chartreuse	1.06	yellow
Drambuie	1.08	gold
Orange curacao	1.08	orange
Sambuca	1.08	white
Triple sec	1.09	white
Amaretto	1.10	light brown
Blue curacao	1.11	blue
Galliano	1.11	golden yellow
Green crème de menthe	1.12	green
White crème de menthe	1.12	white
Coffee liqueur	1.14	dark brown
Dark crème de cacao	1.14	brown
White crème de cacao	1.14	white
Kahlua	1.15	dark brown
Anisette	1.17	white
Grenadine	1.17	red
Crème de cassis	1.18	light brown

Halloween

 SATAN'S WHISKERS

"It just sounds appropriate," explains Robert Hess, mixology enthusiast and operator of www.drinkboy.com. "This is a fairly old cocktail, perhaps created during Prohibition, and while many of the 'wad-o-ingredients' style of drinks from those days are best left behind, I think this drink is quite good."

MIXOLOGY

3/4 oz. gin

3/4 oz. dry vermouth

3/4 oz. sweet vermouth

1/2 oz. orange juice

1/2 oz. Grand Marnier

1 dash orange bitters

Shake with cracked ice, then strain into a chilled cocktail glass.

MIX IT RIGHT: Hess says you should never substitute any other bitters (Angostura or Peychaud) in this drink. "If you don't have orange bitters, then just give it a heavy twist of orange peel."

Election Day

WARD EIGHT

This drink was named after Boston's Ward Eight, which in 1898 was the epicenter of a political struggle—sort of. A candidate for the state legislature, Martin "The Mahatma" Lomansey, was a shoo-in thanks to the efforts of political fixers. This is a perfect drink to prepare at home since bars are closed today in a good number of states. Why? One politician explained it as, "A reminder to citizens and, in some ways, an incentive to vote." Please.

MIXOLOGY

1¹/₂ oz. bourbon

1 oz. orange juice

1 oz. lemon juice

4 dashes grenadine

Pour everything into an ice-filled shaker. Shake well, then strain into a chilled cocktail glass.

Thanksgiving

 ADDAMS'S APPLE

"This drink is very appropriate for Thanksgiving because it tastes like an icy-cold cocktail version of hot apple pie," says Dr. Cocktail (a.k.a. Ted Haigh), operator of www.cocktaildb.com and the person who invented this drink in 1993. "The Addams part—named for the dark-humored cartoonist of that name—is the wicked spicy zing imparted by the uncommon ingredient Pimento Liqueur, a.k.a. Pimento Dram from Jamaica."

MIXOLOGY

2 oz. applejack

1 oz. apple cider

1/4 oz. Pimento Dram

2 dashes orange bitters

Allspice

Combine ingredients in an ice-filled shaker. Shake and strain into a cocktail glass. Garnish with a sprinkle of allspice.

Christmas

 EGGNOG

Forget the milky-sweet crap you buy in plastic jugs at the Safeway. This is what Santa really had in mind when he first told the elves to "Mix up something stiff, okay boys? Got a long night ahead of me." Enough cups of these at a holiday party and someone is sure to suggest a round of strip caroling.

MIXOLOGY

6 large eggs
$3/4$ cup superfine sugar
$1 1/2$ cups brandy
$1/2$ cup rum

4 cups milk
2 cups cream
Nutmeg

Prepare your arm for a serious beating: Separate the eggs and beat the yolks slowly while adding the sugar. Then beat in brandy and rum. (Or two cups of bourbon.) Next, beat in milk and cream. Just before serving, whisk the egg whites until stiff and fold them into the mix. Sprinkle with nutmeg. (Serves 12—or, one per night for 12 days straight.)

New Year's Eve

 THE CHAMPAGNE BOWL

It's the wildest, most bacchanalian night of the year. If you don't want to mess around playing bartender in your own house, opt for serving this huge punch bowl of celebration juice.

MIXOLOGY

4 tbsp. sugar	2 bottles chilled Champagne
Juice of 12 lemons	16 oz. club soda
2 cups brandy	Strawberries
1 cup curacao	Orange slices

Stick an ice block in a punch bowl. Mix sugar with lemon juice and pour over the ice. Add brandy and curacao. Add Champagne—not the stuff you were saving for your 25th wedding anniversary—and club soda. Garnish with strawberries and orange slices. (Serves 20, or two people who don't care about their livers.)

MIX IT RIGHT: When making a Champagne punch, save the Champagne until right before you plan on serving. Bubbles, like your sanity on a holiday, have a funny way of disappearing more quickly than you'd like.

THE PERFECT DRINKING GAME FOR THIS SITUATION: "I Never." Should old acquaintance, sins, or crimes be forgot, this game will refresh your memory. The rules are ridiculously simple: each player takes a turn making an "I Never" statement; anyone who has done what was said must take a drink. For example: If someone says, "I've never been to Brooklyn," and someone in the group has, he/she must drink. That's it. No explanations or apologies necessary; the next person makes his/her statement. Of course, the game can become pretty darn evil, depending on the crowd and how much it wants to share—e.g., "I've never wanted to have sex with someone in this room," or "I've never shoplifted."

Caveat: You may want to avoid statements such as, "I've never killed anybody before," and "I've never had sex with someone using Crisco, a car battery, jumper cables, and a feathered boa."

New Year's Eve ... and You're the Designated Driver

 MOCK CHAMPAGNE

This painless 'pagne comes from food writer Evelyn Cairn, who said: "Who needs alcohol to toast the New Year when this delicious concoction is available?" At any rate, it's cheaper than a jeroboam of Dom Perignon.

MIXOLOGY

4 cups club soda

4 cups ginger ale

3 cups unsweetened white grape juice

All ingredients should be chilled. Combine them in a large pitcher, mix gently, then pour into Champagne flutes right away. (If you're mocking it up alone, use a cup of club soda, a cup of ginger ale, and 3/4 cup white grape juice.)

---

6 THE PERFECT TIME AND SEASON

> *"I know the truth is in between the 1st and the 40th drink."*
> —Tori Amos

It isn't always Miller Time. Sometimes, the perfect libation depends on where you are in the day, week, or year. Just as nobody but Tom Wolfe wears white after Labor Day, no serious drinker will touch a Martini before noon. Here's what you should be ordering . . .

First Thing in the Morning

 GOLDEN DAWN

The little bit of grenadine will sink in the glass, then create a cocktail simulation of a golden sunrise. Hope you're awake enough to enjoy it.

MIXOLOGY

1 1/2 oz. applejack

1 1/2 oz. apricot brandy

1 1/2 oz. dry gin

1 splash orange juice

1 tsp. grenadine

Pour everything except the grenadine into an ice-filled shaker, shake, then strain into a cocktail glass. Now, top it with the grenadine.

Before Lunch

 CAPE CODDER

Up along the Massachusetts coast, they sip these babies slow right before lunch. Why? Because they can.

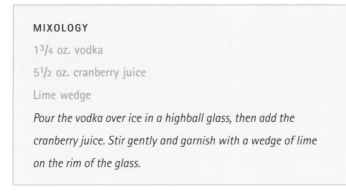

MIXOLOGY

1³/₄ oz. vodka

5¹/₂ oz. cranberry juice

Lime wedge

Pour the vodka over ice in a highball glass, then add the cranberry juice. Stir gently and garnish with a wedge of lime on the rim of the glass.

MIX IT RIGHT: Vodka tastes best when it's colder than Joan Crawford's tit in a brass Victoria's Secret bra. There's no law against storing your best bottle or two in the freezer.

At Lunch

 THE 1950s MARTINI

"The three-Martini lunch is the epitome of American efficiency," said former President Gerald R. Ford. "Where else can you get an earful, a bellyful, and a snootful at the same time?" Excellent point (and watch out for that carpet, Mr. President). In the 1950s, the great American Martini was even seen as a yardstick of a man's business acumen. Take this ad for a sales manager that ran in the *New York Times* in 1956: "Intangible experience, must be able to move effectively at top management level and understand 'Big Business' problems. Should be able to handle 12 Martinis."

MIXOLOGY

1 1/2 oz. dry gin   1 dash orange bitters

1/2 oz. French vermouth   Olive

Stir well with ice, strain into a martini glass, and serve with an olive.

After Your Afternoon Nap

 WHISKEY AND SODA

If you haven't read the diaries of Winston Churchill, here's the condensed version: "Wake up. Drink a bottle of Champagne. Have breakfast, then a whiskey and soda. Take afternoon nap. Have two or three more whiskey and sodas. Eat dinner—with Champagne. Finish up with at least two snifters of brandy. Sleep. Repeat process." I figure that if one of the finest leaders of the twentieth century could snap back to his duties with a whiskey and soda after a short nap, you can, too.

MIXOLOGY

Whiskey

Soda water

Combine the two. Look, you just got up from a nap. Do you really want something complicated?

At the Bar After a Tough Day at Work

 GOLDSTEIN GIBSON

This drink is the "poison of cherce" of my buddy, veteran book editor and gag writer Gary Goldstein. It's perfect for an after-work tune-up, but also many other special occasions, including: "1. Your cable goes out and the only thing your TV can pick up is the local PBS station during pledge week. And 2. You feel the need to celebrate with something strong after your company transfers you to Kandahar."

MIXOLOGY

3 oz. gin

7 cocktail onions

Unopened bottle of dry vermouth

In the words of its inventor: "Fill a shaker with ice. Add gin. Take an unopened bottle of dry vermouth and pass it over the shaker twice. That's as close to the gin as it should get. Shake, pour into glass with cocktail onions. Drink. Enjoy. Order the next one when the first is half gone."

At Dinner

A BOTTLE OF WINE UNDER $15

For most meals it's actually better to have a light wine—you don't want to squander an expensive, complex wine on an ordinary repast. For an outdoor picnic, says Richard Vadya, lead instructor at the New York Restaurant School, a cheap Beaujolais is perfect. Cracking open shellfish? Try a light white wine—which also tend to be very inexpensive. If you're having sauerkraut and pork chops, Vadya suggests a German Riesling. "They're excellent, excellent wines, and you never spend more than $15 on them." You might also check out some increasingly popular "emerging" wine areas—South America, Chile, and Argentina are all making great, sturdy wines. If you're just looking to get schnookered in a hurry, stick with Thunderbird.

After Dinner

 BETWEEN THE SHEETS

This only sounds like a naughty shooter you'd find in a sports bar. This drink was actually invented in Jerusalem at the King David Hotel in the 1930s and was intended to be an after-dinner drink.

MIXOLOGY

3/4 oz. Cognac

3/4 oz. light rum

3/4 oz. Cointreau

1/2 oz. lemon juice

Pour ingredients into a shaker full of ice. Shake and strain into a cocktail glass.

MIX IT RIGHT: For a not-so-sweet version, make this drink with equal parts Cognac, Cointreau, and dry gin.

Late at Night

 NIGHT CAP

Some recommended drinks do not require an explanation. Still need one? Go ask your mother.

MIXOLOGY

2 oz. light rum

1 tsp. powdered sugar

Warm milk

Nutmeg

Put the rum and sugar in a coffee mug, then fill with the warm milk and give it a nice reassuring stir. There, there now. Sprinkle some nutmeg on top.

The Hottest Day of Summer

 ## PINEAPPLE MARTINI

Robert Greene, head bartender at Manhattan's swank Lot 61, has a total of 61 (get it?) varieties of Martini. This refreshing humidity-buster is your best bet when lower Manhattan feels like Whitney Houston's armpits. And while it is slightly sweet, it's still dry enough to qualify as a Martini.

MIXOLOGY

1/4 cup crushed fresh pineapple

2 oz. premium vodka

1 cup sugar

1 cup water

Start by making some simple syrup: mix sugar and water, then boil and stir until sugar is dissolved. Dump the pineapple into a cocktail shaker with ice, then add the vodka and syrup. Shake and strain into a frosted martini glass. If you can have your manservants prepare this for you while you read on the veranda, all the better.

THE DRINK TO AVOID IN THIS SITUATION: Piña Coladas, if for no other reason than it conjures up that stupid song from the '70s.

Hurricane Season

 HURRICANE MARILYN

English bartender Salvatore Calabrese invented this drink after arriving in the British Virgin Islands after Hurricane Marilyn struck. "What was needed was a powerful antidote for the community to help them forget the misery of the hurricane," wrote Calabrese in his book, *Classic Cocktails*. "It worked."

MIXOLOGY

2/3 oz. 54.5 Pusser's rum

2/3 oz. Bacardi rum

1/3 oz. Seagram's V.O.
    Canadian whisky

1/3 oz. Cointreau

2 1/2 oz. cranberry juice

2 1/2 oz. guava juice

3/4 oz. lemon juice

1 or 2 dashes grenadine

Mint sprig

1 fresh strawberry

Kiwi slice

Pour liquids into a shaker and wail on it like Mother Nature. Strain into a chilled highball glass, then garnish with a sprig of mint set into the top of a strawberry. Then add a slice of kiwi fruit on the rim.

A Cool Fall Afternoon

 FALLEN LEAVES

As crisp as a fall day and full of the flavor of the official autumn fruit: the apple. You won't even mind the extra effort involved in tracking down a bottle of calvados (the key ingredient according to Charles Schumann in his book *American Bar*). After all, the air is clean and fresh, and you have nothing to do but walk and hit every liquor emporium within a ten-mile radius.

MIXOLOGY

3/4 oz. calvados (apple brandy)

3/4 oz. sweet vermouth

1/4 oz. dry vermouth

1 splash brandy

Lemon peel

Stir liquids in a mixing glass with ice, then strain into a cocktail glass. Squeeze some lemon into the drink, then garnish with the remainder.

The Coldest Day of Winter

 HOT TODDY

Dark, freezing nights are only good for two things. If sex is out of the question, take the advice of Alex Guzman, a bartender at the Algonquin Hotel in New York, and order a Hot Toddy. This belly-warming drink delivers a double-bang for your buck: The spices will heat you up just as much as the water does.

MIXOLOGY

1 1/2 oz. whiskey or rum

5 oz. hot water

Slice of lemon studded with cloves

Cinnamon

Mix the booze and water in a mug, garnish with the rest.

THE DRINK TO AVOID IN THIS SITUATION: A frozen Strawberry Daiquiri sipped really fast with a straw.

The First Day of Spring

 GIN RICKEY

Invented in the 1890s at Shoemaker's Restaurant in Washington, D.C., when a bartender decided to try out a new warm-weather drink on an unsuspecting lobbyist. That lobbyist? Joe "Colonel Jim" Rickey. Summers go on, as does Rickey's namesake refresher.

MIXOLOGY

1½ oz. gin

1 oz. lime juice

Club soda

Lime wedge

Fill a highball glass with ice, then add the gin and lime juice. Top with soda, stir twice, and garnish with the lime wedge. Alternate technique: Cut a lime in half, squeeze the juice into a highball glass, then drop the whole thing in. Toss in some crushed ice and the gin, then fill with club soda and stir three times.

MIX IT RIGHT: To make a lime wedge, cut off the ends, then cut the lime in half, and then cut those halves into quarters. There. Eight wedges.

7 THE PERFECT PLACE

> *"I'd rather have a free bottle in front of me than a prefrontal lobotomy."*—Tom Waits

Sure, you probably have a favorite bar. And you probably have a favorite drink you always order in that favorite bar. But what if a roving band of kidnappers throws you into the back of their van, shoves a rag soaked with chloroform in your face, drives you to a strange location, and leaves you in front of a strange bar, with nothing but a couple of "free drink" tickets? What are you going to do then? (You'll call the police later. First, you need a drink. You've just been kidnapped!) If you're going to find yourself in strange lands, better learn what the natives are drinking.

San Francisco

 PISCO PUNCH

According to William Grimes's *Straight Up or On the Rocks*, this drink was born in San Francisco in the 1870s, in the Bank Exchange, one of the bars that made up the city's popular "Cocktail Route." The recipe was kept secret for almost 100 years until 1960, when an enterprising historian found one of the surviving Bank bartenders and convinced him to fess up the precise ingredients.

MIXOLOGY

3 oz. Pisco brandy

1 tsp. lime juice

1 tsp. pineapple juice

Pineapple chunks, soaked overnight in sugar syrup

Mix everything with crushed ice and pour into a chilled wine glass.

MIX IT RIGHT: This cocktail has two secret weapons: Pisco brandy, a South American liquor distilled from the sweet Muscat grape, and those syrup-soaked pineapple chunks.

New York City

 MANHATTAN

Be careful—you can't wander too far in the Big Apple without having to change your drink. There are so many cocktails with NYC roots, some streets even have their own cocktail. (Soon, individual studio apartments on the Lower East Side will sport their own, too.) But the quintessential New York City drink is, of course, the ever-popular Manhattan.

MIXOLOGY

2 oz. rye   2 dashes Angostura bitters

1/2 oz. sweet vermouth   Maraschino cherry

Stir with ice and strain into a chilled cocktail glass. Garnish with a maraschino cherry. The rye is vital; other whiskeys won't blend with the vermouth in quite the same way. If you're really stuck, try Canadian Club whisky, which has a good amount of rye in it.

MIX IT RIGHT: More of an outer-borough drinker? Try a Brooklyn: 3 oz. rye, 1 oz. French vermouth, 1 dash Amer Picon, 1 dash Maraschino liqueur. Stir in a mixing pitcher and serve with ice in a rocks glass.

New Orleans

 SAZERAC

Skip the Hurricane—that's New Orleans tourist claptrap. Boozing New Orleans-style is all about ordering up a Sazerac. In the 1850s, a pharmacist named Antoine Peychaud came up with a potion of bitters that he claimed would calm the stomach. Someone—perhaps Peychaud himself—got the idea to mix it with Sazerac & Sons brandy to make the medicine less medicinal. A booze legend was born. If you prefer your Sazeracs on the sweet side, try using bourbon. If you want it the way it was served in the 1850s, use brandy.

MIXOLOGY

1 sugar cube

1 tsp. water

3 dashes Peychaud's Bitters

2 oz. rye bourbon or brandy

Lemon twist

Absinthe substitute
(Pernod, Ricard,
Absente, or a New
Orleans special,
Herbsaint)

Take two old fashioned glasses. Chill one with crushed ice. In the other one, muddle the sugar cube, water, and bitters. Add the bourbon or brandy and stir. Dump the ice from the first glass and pour enough of the Absinthe substitute to coat the inside of the glass. Swirl it around, then dump the extra. Add new ice and the contents of the second glass. Finally, twist a lemon peel over it, but don't add it to the drink.

MIX IT RIGHT: For this New Orleans classic to be the real deal, you've got to find a bottle of Peychaud's Bitters. You can order a bottle through your local liquor retailer, but if you have trouble, contact the Sazerac Company directly at 504-831-9450, or at info@sazerac.com. Your bottle of Peychaud's will come in handy for more than Sazeracs—you can use it as a substitute for Angostura bitters in Manhattans, Old Fashioneds, and Whiskey Sours.

West Virginia

MOUNTAIN MOONSHINE

First there were microbreweries. Then small vanity winemakers. Now, Payton D. Fireman wants to do "boutique booze" by marketing his own brand of "yuppie moonshine," according to the *New York Times*. "You can argue that I'm creating a good way to use the marketplace to drive people out of an illegal business that has been a blight for decades," says Fireman, who sells his corn mash liquor in $9 jars all over West Virginia and Ohio. The difference between his hooch and the time-honored stuff? Fireman actually pays the government tax of $13.50 per 100-proof gallon. (Most moonshine makers skip this step in the distillation process.) As for the taste? Well, it sure ain't triple-distilled boutique vodka. "Of course it's rough," says Fireman. "It's moonshine."

MIXOLOGY

Moonshine is tricky to brew—not to mention illegal—so you're better off buying the stuff. Twist off the metal cap of the mason jar and pour some of the thick, syrupy white stuff into a shot glass. Shoot as quickly as possible. Shoot yourself, if need be.

Philadelphia

 CLOVER CLUB

This drink supposedly originated at the Clover Club, a Quaker City meeting spot of big business types, politicians, writers, and lawyers that used to meet at the Bellevue-Stratford Hotel. In the 1930s, bars across the country delighted upon mixing this Philly export. Years later, the Bellevue fell victim to the mysterious Legionnaire's Disease outbreak in 1976, and the Clover Club fell victim to obscurity. Virtually no one in Philadelphia drinks these anymore, which is a shame. Being a native Philadelphian, I've vowed to bring this drink back, if for no other reason than if this cocktail disappears off the face of the earth, the city's official drink will become Coors Light.

MIXOLOGY

2 oz. gin

1 oz. lemon juice

4 dashes grenadine

1 egg white

Lemon wedge

Shake with cracked ice, then strain into a wine glass. Garnish with lemon wedge.

London

 BLUE HAWAIIAN

Shockingly, the Blue Hawaiian was created in dreary ol' London, at the Zanzibar Club. The revelations don't stop there. Did you know that the Daiquiri was named for a mine near Santiago, Cuba? Or that the Manhattan was first mixed for Winston Churchill's mother? Or that the Sloe Gin Fizz doesn't have any gin in it? Somebody call Oliver Stone.

MIXOLOGY

2 oz. light rum

1 oz. blue curacao

1 oz. sour mix

1 oz. orange juice

1 oz. pineapple juice

Dump everything into a blender with about 3 ounces of ice, press the button, then pour into a chilled collins glass.

Mexico

 TEQUILA ESTILO PANCHO VILLA

Tradition has it that if you're going to drink tequila in a Mexican cantina, you simply have to walk in and exclaim, *"Tequila estilo Pancho Villa, por favor!"* This is roughly translated as, "I'm a goofy gringo! Gimme some tequila!" (Actually, it means, "I'd like some tequila, Pancho Villa style.") The bartender will oblige by handing you a shot, a lime wedge, and some salt.

MIXOLOGY

1 1/2 oz. white tequila

Lime wedge

Coarse kitchen salt

Cradle the lime between the thumb and forefinger of your non-shooting hand. Lick the area of your hand directly above the lime and apply the salt so it sticks. Grab the tequila shot with your other hand. In quick succession: lick the salt, down the tequila, and suck on the lime.

THE DRINK TO AVOID IN THIS SITUATION: Margaritas, which are for tourists.

Cuba

 CUBA LIBRE

Also known as a Rum and Coke, a favorite of college kids everywhere. But back in 1900, the Cuba Libre had a much more prominent place in the pantheon of cocktails. This simple drink was the liquid embodiment of the newfound peace between America and its little cousin to the south, Cuba. And then the bastards had to go and help kill Kennedy.

MIXOLOGY

1^1/$_2$ oz. Bacardi rum

Coca-Cola

Lime wedge

Pour the rum into a collins glass, then add ice and the Coke to fill.

Venezuela

 DUBONNET COCKTAIL

This drink—which simply can't exist without the Dubonnet (herb-fortified French wine)—is remembered for the ad campaign featuring 1950s pinup Pia Zadora. Hipsters of that decade dug the slightly bitter taste and thought the drink was all French and sophisticated-like. Little did they know that it had been around since Prohibition and actually was first concocted in Maracaibo, Venezuela. Ah, youth.

MIXOLOGY

1½ oz. Dubonnet   Lemon twist

1½ oz. gin

Pour liquors into a shaker with ice, then strain into a chilled cocktail glass. Garnish with the lemon twist.

MIX IT RIGHT: To make a lemon twist, put on some Chubby Checker. (Ba-dum. Thank you, I'll be here all week. Try the veal.) Actually, hack off the ends, then scrape the fruit out of the peel with a spoon. Cut the peel lengthwise into quarter-inch strips. When a drink calls for a lemon twist, take the strip, twist it over the drink, rub the inside of the peel around the glass, and drop it in.

Moscow

 VODKA, NEAT

At the Yalta and Teheran conferences following World War II, the attending leaders shared some alcoholic beverages from their native lands. Franklin D. Roosevelt, of course, brought along Martinis. Josef Stalin, however, wasn't too impressed with gin and stuck with his country's finest achievement—vodka. "It had warmed them in the desperate hours of Stalingrad's defense," writes William Grimes in *Straight Up or On the Rocks.* "This was no ordinary spirit. It was Bolshevism in liquid form." Communism may have died, but a good stiff vodka in a cold Russian winter certainly hasn't.

> **MIXOLOGY**
> Vodka
> Shot glass
> *Pour vodka into a shot glass. Shoot.*

THE DRINK TO AVOID IN THIS SITUATION: A Moscow Mule (vodka, ginger beer, and lime), because no true Soviet will know what the hell you're talking about. The Mule is strictly a red-blooded American concoction, as are all other vodka cocktails.

Desert Island

 BACARDI SAOCO

This drink depends on the gods sinking a cargo ship full of Bacardi a short distance away. Also, it might be tough finding a refrigerator on the island to chill the coconut. Hell, you may not even have coconuts. But at the very least, this recipe will give your feverish mirage-fantasies a dose of realism that they would otherwise lack.

MIXOLOGY

1 coconut

1 bottle Bacardi Carta Blanca (Light–Dry) rum

Sugar

Chill the coconut for 24 hours, then cut open a hole and pour in the rum. Add sugar to taste.

MIX IT RIGHT: Make a primitive form of island booze by cutting a hole in a coconut, pouring in 3 or 4 teaspoons of sugar, then plugging the hole. Nature takes its course, and when the plug blows out of the nut, your coconut milk has fully fermented.

Office

 COFFEE COCKTAIL

Careful readers will notice that coffee does not appear in this recipe. That's because this drink—when mixed properly—should resemble a cup of joe, only without the steam, according to *My New Cocktail Book*. This drink came into vogue during Prohibition, when it wasn't a smart idea to be seen sipping booze.

MIXOLOGY

1/3 part port wine

1/6 part brandy

1 splash curacao

1 egg yolk

1 tsp. Gum syrup

Pour the ingredients into a coffee mug full of ice, mix well, and serve.

Prison

 TOILET BOWL PUNCH

Prisons, military schools, nunneries—Toilet Bowl Punch is a classic, no matter where you serve it. Get the word out to your people: You need fruit juice, a small garbage bag, and some yeast. The first two aren't tough—you probably got somebody in the kitchen watching your back anyway. The yeast is tricky, though. If nobody can score that for you, slip a slice of Wonder in your pocket at chow time and let it get moldy. Combine the juice and the yeast (or moldy bread, which is the same thing essentially) into the garbage bag, then stash it someplace. Many cons prefer the toilet. After a while, it'll ferment and you'll be able to get your booze on.

MIXOLOGY

Fruit juice

Yeast

Small garbage bag

Combine, then hide. Drink when fermented. Watch your back.

Airplane

THE BUCK STOPS HERE

Remember the story about the jerk who got so schnookered, he mistook a snack cart for the potty? Or the one about Peter Buck, the R.E.M. guitarist who got so blitzed on a flight from England to Seattle on British Airways that he upended snack carts and screamed, "You're just a fucking pilot! I am R.E.M.!" Unless you want to be ill remembered—or apply for membership in R.E.M.—keep off the airline hooch and try this tasty mocktail instead. It's made with ingredients stocked by most airlines.

MIXOLOGY

4 oz. cranberry juice

4 oz. grape juice

Club soda to fill

Lime wedge

Serve over ice in a plastic cup; garnish with a wedge of lime.

Beauty Salon

 THE PLATINUM BLONDE

Pretty much the only bar in L.A. where you can get a legal blow . . . dry,
Beauty Bar is a watering hole made up to look like a 1960s-era beauty
salon, reportedly frequented by David Schwimmer and Marisa Tomei.

MIXOLOGY

2 oz. Stoli vodka

1 oz. Malibu rum

1 1/2 oz. pineapple juice

1/2 oz. soda water

1/2 oz. 7-Up

Maraschino cherry

*Mix all ingredients in
a 6-ounce martini
glass, then garnish
with a cherry.*

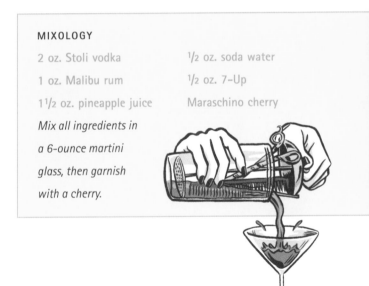

Star Trek Convention

VULCAN MIND PROBE

Hundreds of teary-eyed Trekkies consoled themselves with this drink after William Shatner—a.k.a. James Tiberius Kirk—told them to "get a life." After swallowing this in one gulp, you may doubt your ability to live long and/or prosper. And you certainly won't be able to do that weird Vulcan greeting thing with your fingers.

> **MIXOLOGY**
>
> 1/2 oz. 151-proof rum
>
> 1/2 oz. peppermint schnapps
>
> 1/2 oz. Bailey's Irish cream
>
> *Layer in a shot glass in the preceding order, then serve with a straw.*

DRINKS TO AVOID IN THIS SITUATION: The "Klingon Sling," "Borg Assimilation," and "Sex on an Alien Beach with Worf."

Sip your drink if:

Bones says, "He's dead, Jim," or points out that he's a doctor, not a [blank].

Kirk violates the prime directive, orders phasers on stun, gets the girl, outwits a computer, saves the day with a stirring speech, or bluffs his way out.

Spock shows emotion, uses the Vulcan nerve pinch, says "illogical," "fascinating," or "indeed."

Scotty complains about the warp speed requested or negates space and time.

Chekov says, "But Keptin . . ."

Sulu sets the course.

Uhura says "hailing frequencies open" or sings.

The weapons are suddenly powerless, the transporter is suddenly inoperative, the Dilithium crystals are screwed up, the shields are about to collapse, or they happen upon a new planet that is "much like Earth."

Chug your drink if:

Kirk does not get the girl.

Sulu gets a sword.

A major character dies or is assumed dead.

Lt. Leslie speaks.

Someone makes a historical reference to the twentieth century.

The crew meets God and he/she turns out to be a child, insane,
or an insane child.

8 THE PERFECT DRINK THROUGHOUT HISTORY

> *"When I read about the evils of drinking, I gave up reading."*
> —Henny Youngman

Every era has its drink. The man in the gray flannel suit was fully armed with briefcase in one hand, Martini in the other. Knights held mugs of mead close to armored chests. Dot com cubicle survivors wrap their paws around mugs of Pabst Blue Ribbon and shot glasses of Jim Beam in cheap dives just a few blocks away from their overpriced apartments. In case you ever tumble into a Way-Back Machine, you'd better know what to order. Here's what people were drinking in . . .

The Revolutionary War

FLIP

"Our sturdy brass-lined forebears actually drank it!" marvels Irvin S. Cobb in his 1934 eponymous mixology book. "They drank it for breakfast!" No one knows why it's called Flip, but considering the contents—beer, molasses, and rum—perhaps it has something to do with what this drink will do to a human stomach. Cobb claims this warm punch was the "earliest chronicled American potation." He adds: "The interesting concoction in question dated back to before the Revolution. Personally, I'm inclined to think it may have had quite a good deal to do with bringing on the Revolution."

MIXOLOGY

Strong home-brewed beer   Rum

Crude molasses   1 hot poker

Combine the first three into a pitcher—the molasses will sweeten the beer—and warm it by plunging a red-hot poker into it.

MIX IT RIGHT: Some colonial-era boozehounds used to crack a raw goose egg into their Flip, turning it into A Yard of Flannel.

The Mid-19th Century

 TOM AND JERRY PUNCH

Professor Jerry Thomas invented this drink while bartending at the Planter's House Hotel in St. Louis, one of the country's most famous hotels. Originally, though, Thomas dubbed it a Copenhagen, since rum-and-egg drinks were huge in Denmark. But many punch-loving fans at Planter's House started calling it a "Jerry Thomas," in honor of its creator. Over the years, this became "Tom and Jerry," and eventually, "Tom and Jerry" became an animated cat and mouse chase that stretches into infinity.

MIXOLOGY

5 pounds sugar

12 eggs, separated

6 oz. Jamaican rum

1 1/2 tsp. ground cinnamon

1/2 tsp. ground cloves

1/2 tsp. ground allspice

Brandy

Nutmeg

1 gallon boiling water

"Beat the whites of the eggs to a stiff froth and the yolks until they are as thin as water, then mix together and add the spice and rum, thicken with sugar until the mixture attains the consistency of light batter," writes Professor Jerry Thomas in his landmark 1928 drink book The Bon Vivant's Companion or, How to Mix Drinks. *When you're about to serve it to a customer, take a bar glass and add a tablespoon of the above mixture. Add one wine glass full of brandy and then fill the rest with boiling water. Top with nutmeg.*

MIX IT RIGHT: Thomas adds that you might substitute a mixture of "one-half brandy, one-fourth Jamaica rum, and one-fourth Santa Cruz rum" instead of plain brandy. "This compound is usually mixed and kept in a bottle and a wineglassful is used for each tumbler of Tom and Jerry."

The Old West

 THE YELLOW DAISY COCKTAIL

Richard William Clark, a.k.a. "Deadwood Dick," was the quintessential cowboy. He worked the Pony Express, guarded stagecoaches, and inspired a series of 64 western novels (the Deadwood Dick series) by E. K. Wheeler. He hung with Wild Bill Hickok, Calamity Jane, and Buffalo Bill. And when he kicked off his spurs and settled back before a blazing campfire, Clark drank a few of these babies—an Old West version of the latter-day Martini. I don't recommend drinking this in front of a blazing campfire, though. Your ice will melt too fast.

MIXOLOGY

2 oz. gin

2 oz. French vermouth

1 oz. Grand Marnier

1 dash Pernod

Pour into an ice-filled shaker, add a dash of Pernod, shake, then strain into a martini glass.

World War I

 FRENCH 75

This drink was named after the artillery guns used by the French during the Great War. Some historians also believe that the French 75 (the drink) gave French field officers the courage to charge into battle with their French 75s (the weapon.) At any rate, our American boys discovered this cocktail and brought it back with them at war's end.

MIXOLOGY

1 1/2 oz. gin

3/4 oz. lemon juice

1/2 tsp. powdered sugar

4 oz. chilled Champagne

Lemon twist

Mix the gin, lemon juice, and sugar in a collins glass that is half-filled with ice. Fill the rest of the way with the Champagne, then garnish with the twist.

MIX IT RIGHT: Try this alternate version: 4 oz. Champagne, 1/4 oz. gin, 1/4 oz. Cointreau, 1/4 oz. lemon juice. Shake everything but the Champagne with cracked ice, then strain into a chilled flute. Top with the Champagne and garnish with lemon twist.

Prohibition

 RYE AND GINGER

Rye and Ginger was so popular during Prohibition, writes William Grimes in *Straight Up or On the Rocks*, that sales of ginger ale doubled between 1920 and 1928. John O'Hara described a type of Rye and Ginger in a scene at a country club in *Appointment in Samarra*. "The liquor, that is the rye, was all about the same: most people brought drug store rye on prescriptions (the physicians who were club members saved 'scrips' for their patients) and cut it with alcohol and colored water. It was not poisonous and it got you tight, which was all that was required of it and that could be said for it."

> **MIXOLOGY**
>
> Rye
>
> Ginger ale
>
> *Procure some illegal rye—either from Canada or from a doctor's office, where it was supposed to be used for "medicinal purposes only"—and cut it with ginger ale, to taste, over ice in an old fashioned glass.*

DRINKS TO AVOID IN THIS ERA: Anything made with booze produced by Chicago's "Terrible Gennas." These six brothers, according to Gus Russo's *The Outfit*, a history of organized crime in Chicago, used industrial alcohol to make illegal hooch. The Gennas "colored it with various toxins known to cause psychosis and called it bourbon, Scotch, rye . . . whatever. Glycerin was added to make the concoction smooth enough to be swallowed." The stuff could quite literally make you go blind. Ironically, Prohibition—meant to save innocent Americans from the evils of drink—resulted in the creation of highly toxic booze. Nice going, Volstead.

The Repeal of Prohibition

 VERMOUTH CASSIS

Hell, what wasn't popular when the U.S. Government finally pushed the wooden stake into the heart of the ill-conceived Volstead Act? In 1934, *Esquire* magazine published a list of "The Ten Best Cocktails," which were: the Old Fashioned, the Dry Martini, the Ward Eight, the Daiquiri, the Champagne Cocktail, Planter's Punch, the Harvest Moon, the Old Fashioned Dutch, the Vodka Cocktail, and the Vermouth Cassis. This was the age when vermouth was still your friend—hell, anything but bathtub gin was your friend. Hence, here's a tip of the hat to that much-maligned spirit.

MIXOLOGY

3 oz. dry vermouth

1 oz. crème de cassis

Club soda

Mix the liquors together in an ice-filled highball glass, then fill with club soda.

The 1950s

MAI TAI

"Mai tai—ro ae!" Translation: Dude, that's a lot of rum! No, actually, that's Tahitian for "Out of this world—the best." Polynesian cocktail god Trader Vic (a.k.a. Victor Bergeron) first mixed this drink in 1944 at his restaurant, Hinky Dink's, in Oakland, California. "I took down a bottle of 17-year-old rum," explained Bergeron years later. "It was J. Wray Nephew from Jamaica; surprisingly golden in color, medium bodied but with the rich pungent flavor particular to the Jamaican blends. I took a fresh lime, added some orange curacao from Holland, a dash of Rock Candy Syrup, and a dollop of French orgeat, for its subtle almond flavor. A generous amount of shaved ice and vigorous shaking by hand produced the marriage I was after. I stuck in a branch of fresh mint and gave two of them to Ham and Carrie Guild, friends from Tahiti who were there that night." Carrie uttered the phrase and a cocktail revolution was born.

Vic's offhand rum creation would become a favorite of men in gray flannel suits and their well-coifed wives across the country, helping to kick off a Polynesian food-and-booze craze in the 1950s.

MIXOLOGY

1 oz. light rum	1½ tsp. French orgeat
1 oz. dark rum	(almond syrup)
½ oz. curacao	Lime peel
1½ tsp. simple syrup	Mint sprig

Mix everything except the lime and mint in an ice-filled shaker, then pour into a chilled old fashioned glass. Garnish with lime and mint.

MIX IT RIGHT: Ask a bartender today for a Mai Tai and they'll probably give you something that tastes like Tropical Kool-Aid spiked with rum. That ain't my tai, partner. Your best bet is to hit a first-class bar where they know what French orgeat is—it's a sweet syrup made from almonds, sugar, and rose water—or try to lay in a bottle for yourself and make it at home. (If you can't find orgeat, try to find an almond syrup at any high-end culinary shop.) Or hit a real Trader Vic's restaurant—there are 17 of them scattered across the globe.

The 1960s

 HEMP VODKATINI

Ah, the 1960s. While Mom and Pop were still stirring water and blended whiskey in the den, little Buck and Judy were experimenting with a blend of a different kind: namely, marijuana leaves combined with rolling papers. No cocktail stood a chance of being embraced by the Mary Jane generation, so we've retroactively designated one for them, thanks to a modern-day concoction called Hemp Vodka. Made in England, Hemp Vodka is a triple distilled vodka made with real hemp seed (*Cannabis Sativa L.,* to be exact). This doesn't mean that man has found a way to distill booze from pot; the seeds are added during the bottling process just to give it a peaceful, easy-ridin' flavor. But don't drink too much, or else you'll get a wicked case of the munchies.

> **MIXOLOGY**
>
> *To order, there's no need to find that shady guy who used to sell you joints in college. Check out www.cannabisvodka.co.uk. After you lay in a bottle, store it in the freezer. Shake with ice and strain into a martini or rocks glass.*

The 1970s

LONG ISLAND ICED TEA

This is not just a Long Island crack. It was actually first mixed there in the 1970s by Robert "Rosebud" Butt at the Oak Beach Inn in Hampton Bays. The purpose of a Long Island Iced Tea, of course, is to pack as much booze into a cocktail that tastes suspiciously like an ordinary glass of iced tea. (There is no iced tea, as you can see, in the ingredient list.)

MIXOLOGY

¹/₂ oz. vodka	¹/₂ oz. triple sec
¹/₂ oz. rum	¹/₂ oz. tequila
¹/₂ oz. gin	Coca-Cola

Shake all of the spirits in an ice-filled shaker, then strain into a highball glass. Fill with cola. Never shake with the cola inside—you'll ruin the effect.

MIX IT RIGHT: Want to be an outlaw? Make this drink using one ounce doses of each of the base spirits. In some states, drinks with more than four ounces of hard liquor are prohibited in bars and restaurants. Of course, there's probably a good reason for that.

The 1980s

 SEX ON THE BEACH

Men Without Hats. A Flock of Seagulls haircut. Velcro. Sex on the Beach. Thank God the 1980s are long over. But then again, that decade of wretched Reagan excess was primed for a nostalgia-fueled comeback. When it comes full on, this is what you'll be drinking.

MIXOLOGY

(Beachfront Condo Version)

1 oz. vodka	1 1/2 oz. pineapple juice
1/2 oz. Midori	1 1/2 oz. cranberry juice
1/2 oz. Chambord	cocktail

Pour everything into an ice-filled shaker and shake, then strain into a chilled highball glass.

(Summer Share Version)

1/2 oz. peach schnapps	3 oz. pineapple juice
1/2 oz. vodka	3 oz. cranberry juice

Pour everything right into a highball glass with ice. Stir sloppily.

The 1990s

 FRENCH MARTINI

The '90s ended with a weird temporal hiccup that revived the Rat Pack ethos: swing hard, drink harder, and wear sharp-looking suits. Thanks to movies like *Swingers* and bands like the Squirrel Nut Zippers, old-fashioned drinks—like the Old Fashioned—were all the rage in bars from New York to L.A. If your grandfather drank it, it was cool. Martinis came back from the dead—and spawned an entirely new species of drink, what with Apple Martinis and Chocolate Martinis and Zagnut Martinis and Mayonnaise Martinis. Sidecars peeled out of obscurity. This spirit of cocktail rediscovery has continued until the present, hence this book. Here's one of the better nouveau Martinis, enjoyed by Nicole Kidman, Mark Wahlberg, Milla Jovovich, and even Joan Collins.

MIXOLOGY

2 oz. Stoli orange

2 oz. Lillet

Pour both in a shaker filled with ice. Shake, then strain into a chilled martini glass.

The Eve of Y2K

 MILLENNIUM COCKTAIL

According to *Playboy* food writer John Mariani, this is what New Yorkers were swilling at the Blackbird Restaurant on New Year's Eve of 1999, not far from Times Square. At Times Square, Dick Clark was sipping formaldehyde.

MIXOLOGY

1½ oz. Courvoisier Millennium Cognac

¼ oz. Hiram Walker orange liqueur

2 dashes Angostura bitters

1½ oz. pineapple juice

Orange twist

Combine all of the ingredients (except the twist, genius) in a shaker with ice cubes. Shake until cold, then strain into a martini glass. Now you can use the twist as garnish.

Rightthisverymoment

 CAIPIRINHA

It came from Brazil and is invading American and European bars every-where. Bartenders here will probably charge you close to $10 for this drink-of-the-moment, which is odd, considering that one translation of "Caipirinha" (pronounced *kay-i-peer-een-ya*) is "the farmer's drink." Legend has it that Henry Ford was frustrated with all of the South American workers who preferred to sip Caipirinhas than process the tin and rubber for his cars. Sip yours down and know you're doing your part to thumb your nose at the capitalist pigs.

MIXOLOGY

2 oz. cachaça

1 oz. club soda

1 tbsp. superfine guar

Half a lime, peeled and
    sliced into thin rounds

Sugar cane stick

Lime wedge

Muddle the lime and sugar in a rocks glass, then fill with ice. Pour the cachaça and club soda over ice. Serve with a stick of sugar cane and lime garnish.

MIX IT RIGHT: The secret ingredient is the cachaça, a 500-year-old Brazilian spirit that's a close cousin to tequila but distilled from sugar cane instead of the blue agave plant. If you can't lay your paws on a bottle of cachaça, you can substitute high-end vodka, in which case you'll be making a Caipiroshka. Substitute white rum and it's a Caipirissima.

9 WHAT TO DRINK IF YOU'RE TIRED OF . . .

> *"Candy is dandy, but liquor is quicker."*—Ogden Nash

You belly up to the bar. The bartender raises an eyebrow. "The usual?" he asks. You nod. Within moments, "the usual" is sitting on a clean white napkin square in front of your nose. You sip at it until it's empty. The bartender raises an eyebrow. "Another one?" You nod. Within moments, another "usual" is sitting on a clean white napkin square in front of your nose. You sip at it. Times passes. Flowers wilt. Ah, the ennui. "Another one?" You nod.

What are you, a broken record? Of course not. You just didn't know you had other choices. Here are some delicious alternatives to . . .

Long Island Iced Teas

 EYES WIDE SHUT

Amateur mixologist Jeff Sewell, who invented this drink, says that if it's mixed correctly, you shouldn't taste any alcohol at all. (Which, of course, is why so many people dig Long Island Iced Teas.)

MIXOLOGY

$^1/_2$ oz. Southern Comfort $^1/_2$ oz. cranberry juice

$^1/_2$ oz. Crown Royal whisky   1 splash grenadine

$^1/_2$ oz. Amaretto   Orange slice

$^1/_2$ oz. orange juice   Maraschino cherry

$^1/_2$ oz. pineapple juice

Pour all liquids into a shaker full of crushed ice. Shake, then strain into a cocktail glass full of ice. Garnish with the orange slice and cherry.

MIX IT RIGHT: If you're pouring a series of drinks from the same shaker, line up your glasses end to end. Pour each drink only halfway, then go back and even up the contents. This ensures that every glass receives the same amount.

Gin and Tonics

 THE AVIATION

Still the same gin, but the boring tonic water is jettisoned in favor of the sweet Maraschino—a clear-but-not-cloying Italian liqueur—and a bit of sour from the lemon juice. *GQ* drinks columnist Terry Sullivan theorized that this Depression-era favorite was named for air travel because back in the 1930s, flying was still a rather dangerous proposition. Much like this drink.

MIXOLOGY

2 oz. gin

1 oz. lemon juice

1/2 to 1 oz. Maraschino liqueur or simple syrup

Pour everything into a shaker filled with ice, then strain into a chilled cocktail glass.

Manhattans

THE HOMESKILLET

"This sling on a Manhattan was actually created when I was living in Manhattan and just beginning to play with cocktails as a hobby," says amateur mixologist Chris Holst. "Having recently tracked down an elusive bottle of Maraschino to make my first Aviation, one thing led to another and this concoction was the result. A friend of discerning tastes christened it the 'Homeskillet.' It has gathered somewhat of a following. If only Maraschino were not so rare behind commercial bars."

MIXOLOGY

1½ oz. Canadian whisky   1 dash bitters

½ oz. sweet vermouth   Maraschino cherry

¼ oz. Maraschino liqueur

Shake the first three contents over ice, add the bitters, then garnish with a cherry.

MIX IT RIGHT: If you want a less sweet and more spicy version, substitute bourbon for the Canadian whisky.

Piña Coladas

 PASSION FRUIT

"This is a sweet, refreshing drink for the summer," says Scott Young, president of Extremebartending.com. "It's a good drink to serve someone who can't make up their mind."

MIXOLOGY

1/2 oz. Midori

1/2 oz. white rum

2 oz. cranberry juice

2 oz. pineapple juice

2 oz. 7-Up

Lemon wedge

In a tall glass filled with ice, add the above ingredients and give them a gentle stir. Garnish with the lemon.

Rum and Cokes

LOCO RUMBA

Rum and Coke purists—yes, they do exist—will tell you that the drink is solely dependent on Coca-Cola; only the morally depraved or confused college student would ever mix something called a "Rum and Pepsi." Likewise, this newfangled cocktail is solely dependent on its soda component: Loco Soda, a surprisingly spicy-hot beverage that comes in five varieties (lime, mango, raspberry, blackberry, and watermelon) and has quietly become a hit at some Manhattan clubs and restaurants. It was invented by a chef named Ron Crismon, who was bored with ordinary soft drinks and decided to create his own with lime juice, lemon juice, and fresh-brewed chili peppers. "Studies have shown that people with chili peppers in their diet have six times more sex than people without," explained Crismon to the *New York Times*.

MIXOLOGY

1½ oz. light rum

3½ oz. Loco Mango

1 splash grenadine

Lime wheel

Pour rum over ice in a wine glass, then add the Loco. Add grenadine, then garnish with the lime or lemon. The New York Times *recommends that you serve this drink with mariachi music.*

MIX IT RIGHT: Right now, you can find Loco Sodas in high-end grocery stores across the country, mainly in the northeast and south. To find a location near you, check out www.locosoda.com.

Margaritas

TEQUILA AND SQUIRT

Down in Mexico, they don't drink their tequila with crushed ice and fruit; they either shoot it, or they dump it into a can of Squirt. Squirt is one of those second tier—no, actually fourth or fifth tier—soft drinks. What differentiates it from, say, Sprite or 7-Up is that it has a distinct grape-fruit taste and it goes great with tequila for some reason, according to Terry Sullivan in *GQ*. "It's as easy as a Jack and Coke roadie, can be mixed in the back of a truck, and the result is a mighty close cousin to a Margarita at a tenth of the effort," he writes.

MIXOLOGY

1 can of Squirt

1 1/2 oz. white tequila

Open the can, take a swallow or two, then pour in the tequila.
Yes, right into the can.

Martinis

LONE TREE

A genetic hybrid of a Bronx and a Martini, the Lone Tree definitely stands apart, with more vermouth than the usual Martini—and also more flavor. This is definitely not a drink for those Martini lovers who'd like nothing better than to see a bottle of vermouth tied to a tree and shot.

> **MIXOLOGY**
>
> 3/4 oz. gin
>
> 3/4 oz. dry vermouth
>
> 3/4 oz. sweet vermouth
>
> 3–4 dashes orange bitters
>
> Olive
>
> *Pour everything except the olive into a shaker filled with ice. Shake it up, then strain into a chilled cocktail glass. Pop the olive in there.*

MIX IT RIGHT: Olives for Martinis and Lone Trees should be medium-sized pitted green ones. Pimientos are a waste of time—opt for olives without.

Tropical Cocktails with Rum

 SINGAPORE SLING

Here's one of the few tropical drinks that doesn't involve rum. A "sling," by the way, just means a sweet drink made with brandy, whiskey, or gin. A lemon is usually involved, too. "A Singapore Gin Sling is one of the world's finest drinks," proclaimed the *New York Sun* on August 21, 1934. "It cannot be slung together by any bartender. It must be fondled and delicately adjusted."

MIXOLOGY

2 oz. gin

1 oz. cherry brandy

1 splash benedictine

3/4 oz. lemon juice

Club soda to fill

Lemon slice

Mint sprig

Pour the first four ingredients into an ice-filled shaker, along with a splash of club soda. Shake it until it sings. Strain into a chilled highball glass, then add some ice cubes and club soda to fill. Garnish with the lemon and mint.

---

⑩ SPECIAL SITUATIONS

"The whole world is about three drinks behind."
—Humphrey Bogart

Most of the cocktails in this book fit into neat, easily identifiable categories and/or situations. There comes a time, however, when life isn't so neat or easily identifiable. Hell, life is never neat or easily identifiable. Why were you wasting time reading the rest of this book? This is the chapter you want. These are the drinks that deal with the random, unexpected, and quirky situations where . . .

You Want to Make the Second Easiest Cocktail in the World

 HIGHBALL

"Highball" is not synonymous with "cocktail." According to legend, the name comes from American railroad engineers, who used to raise a ball on a pole if a certain train was running late. (Legend does not say if this was meant to represent a lanced testicle, hoisted high.) At any rate, a "highball" loosely translates into "a drink in a hurry," and what could be easier than slapping together Scotch, ice, and water, mixing quickly and sipping slowly? Anything less would simply be Scotch on the rocks and that simply ain't no cocktail, friend. A *Life* magazine poll in 1947 revealed that 30 percent of American drinkers wrapped their paws around a Highball, beating Martinis, Manhattans, and all other forms of cocktail hollow.

But be warned that hard-core drinkers look upon Highballs with disdain. "Water may be useful in putting out fires, floating ferryboats, making tea, washing cars and bodies, sustaining vegetables, cooling engines, and supporting soap manufacturers, [but it] doesn't belong in a drink," rants Ted Shane in his 1950 *Bar Guide*. "Only idiots would put it in soups or soft drinks and only dishonest people put it in milk, gas, or wine—so why put it in liquor?"

Still, when you're in a fix and need a quick nip, you can't go wrong with a time-saver. Want other Highballs? Whip up a Gin and Tonic—known in my household as a G&T—and gussy it up by smearing a lime wedge along the rim of your glass. Try an Irish Cooler, which is simply Irish Whiskey and club soda, with a little lemon garnish if you're feeling zippy. A 7&7 is Seagram's 7 Crown Whisky and 7-Up. A Horse's Neck is bourbon and ginger ale and is traditionally garnished with an impossibly long spiral-cut lemon peel that reaches from the drink's top down deep to the bottom of the glass. But if you're sitting there trying to cut a long-ass lemon peel, why the hell are you drinking a Highball?

MIXOLOGY

$1^1/_2$ oz. whiskey

2 ice cubes

Soda water to fill

Combine all three in a rocks glass.

You Want to Make the Easiest Cocktail in the World

 ## SCREWDRIVER

Legend has it that this drink was first mixed by an American oilman who was in Iran and couldn't find a swizzle stick to stir his vodka and orange juice. Luckily, he had another tool handy: a Black & Decker Power Drill. (Kidding, kidding.) Even school children have access to the two key ingredients here: orange juice and vodka. A Screwdriver's preparation couldn't be more rudimentary, and mistakes are simple to remedy. Too weak? Add more vodka. Too strong? Add more juice. Some Screwdrivers, in fact, go on forever that way.

> **MIXOLOGY**
>
> Some vodka
>
> Some orange juice
>
> *Try to make it more orange juice than vodka. Mix to taste.*

You're Having Trouble Pronouncing Words

TOM COLLINS

It's all about the hard T and the hard C. "A fellow can still say 'Tom Collins' quite distinctly long after he has lost the ability to pronounce," writes novelist and Kentucky-born tippler Irwin S. Cobb in his 1934 booze guide. The Collins—in all of its varied forms—is a classic cocktail that dates back to the early 1800s and barman (duh) John Collins, who tilted the bottles at Limmer's Hotel in London. His original mix called for a base of dry Dutch gin. Later, someone decided to replace that with a gin with the brand name Old Tom, hence the "Tom Collins." The drink was wildly popular with American flyboys during World War I, who brought Mr. Collins stateside after the war, and it soon became a beloved classic.

MIXOLOGY

2–3 oz. gin

1 1/2 oz. lemon juice

1/2 oz. sugar syrup

Club soda

Maraschino cherry (optional)

Mix first three ingredients in a tall collins glass, fill with the soda, and add the cherry—if you want. (Some purists think the cherry is an unnecessary add-on.)

DRINKS TO AVOID IN THIS SITUATION: Sssssingapore Ssssllll-ings, Noilly Prats, and pousse-cafés.

MIX IT RIGHT: There are many branches in the Collins family tree. Want a Jack Collins? Use applejack instead of gin. Mike Collins? Use Irish Whiskey. Sandy Collins? Scotch. Pedro Collins? Rum. Brandy Collins? You-know-what.

You Have a Buck and Change

 BEER FROM THE TAP

Unfortunately, you can no longer slap down a handful of coins on top of a bar and receive a tumbler full of smooth amber fluid in return. Any spirit that costs less than two bucks is sure to be rot-gut rail swill, except maybe those that come in a test tube. And if you're down to your last couple of dollars, the last thing you need is booze in a test tube. No, the only reasonable way to go is to order up a mug or pint of beer from a tap. Almost any beer tastes good coming from a tap—this is why beer lovers still go to bars (or save up their nickels and buy a home tap system).

Don't bother with the trendy bars with microbrews on tap. Find a nice quiet neighborhood joint, with wood paneling on the walls, chipped white tile with little boomerang shapes on the floor, maybe even a little stamped tin on the ceiling. Ask if the décor has changed since 1950. If it has, split. If they look at you funny when you say the word "décor," stay. Sit on the puffy vinyl-covered stool and help yourself to the shelled peanuts in the bowl. Order a mug of whatever strikes your fancy. (If it's the right kind of neighborhood bar, you won't have much choice.) Sip and enjoy, and strike up a conversation with the bartender, who will most likely be beefing, balding, and named Sal. I'll take a cheap tap beer

in one of these places—and its vintage sights, colors, and conversations—
over the swankiest Greenwich Village Martini spot any day.

FIVE CLASSIC BEERS . . . AMAZINGLY, STILL ON TAP!

- **Schlitz**
- **Pabst Blue Ribbon**
- **Rheingold Extra Dry Lager**
- **Schmidt's**
- **Yuengling**

*But you don't have to hunt down blasts from the past. Hell, even
Budweiser tastes good when it's cold and served from a tap.*

DRINKS TO AVOID IN THIS SITUATION: Attention college students and recently downsized dot-commers: If you're flat broke, don't hit
the nail polish remover or rubbing alcohol. Those are labeled "industrial
alcohols" for a reason—namely, the methanol is so harsh, it will work you
into blindness, paralysis, or an early grave.

You Want to Embarrass Your Friend

 WOO WOO

For when your buddy asks, "You need anything from the bar?" (God, you're a dick.) The only downside: You'll have to drink it.

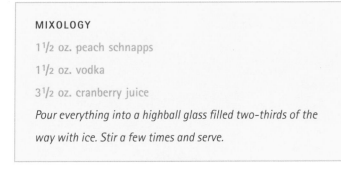

MIXOLOGY

1$^{1}/_{2}$ oz. peach schnapps

1$^{1}/_{2}$ oz. vodka

3$^{1}/_{2}$ oz. cranberry juice

Pour everything into a highball glass filled two-thirds of the
way with ice. Stir a few times and serve.

You're in a Scatological Frame of Mind

 TIDY BOWL

This novelty drink resembles the waters a certain miniature-sized man once navigated in the interest of clean American toilets. One bartender in Norfolk, Virginia, was fond of completing the effect by floating a raisin on top of the shot.

MIXOLOGY

2 oz. blue curacao

Splash pineapple juice

Pour blue curacao in a shaker filled with ice. Strain into a shot glass, then add a splash of pineapple juice.

You're on Tour with Don Rickles

 DIRTY DOG

According to Rickles's tour rider—obtained by TheSmokingGun.com—the preeminent wisenheimer demands the following in his dressing room: 1 bottle each of "Absolute" [sic] or Stoli, Scotch, Cognac, dry vermouth, red wine, white wine; also 6 rocks glasses, assorted cocktail mixers and assorted cocktail fruit, including lemons, limes, olives, and onions. You can make many a cocktail based on this impressive array of Rat Pack–era supplies, but this drink says it best.

MIXOLOGY

1 oz. Cognac

1 1/2 oz. vodka

5 oz. orange juice

1 oz. cranberry juice

Crushed ice

Put all ingredients into a blender, blend, then pour into a highball glass.

You Need to Watch Something Go Up in Flames

 BLUE BLAZER

The world's first—and by far, flashiest—flaming cocktail was invented in the early nineteenth century by bartending legend Jerry Thomas. This is perhaps one of the toughest drinks to mix, if not for the end result, then for the pyrotechnical display beforehand.

MIXOLOGY

4 oz. Scotch

3 oz. boiling water

1 tsp. powdered sugar

Lemon peel

First, you'll need two silver mugs with handles; nothing huge or heavy. Pour the Scotch into one mug, the boiling water into the other. Ignite the Scotch. Now comes the tricky part: pour the flaming Scotch into the other mug, then back and forth, at least four or five times. If done correctly, there should be one continuous stream of liquid flame passing from one mug to

> *the other. After the flame dies and receives the proper oohs and aahhhs, pour the Scotch and water into a wine glass (heated would be nice), then top with the powdered white sugar and garnish with the lemon peel.*

🍸 MIX IT RIGHT: Worried about the Blue Blazer? You could try an easier flaming drink called The Flambeau. Take 2 oz. Captain Morgan rum, 1 oz. Chambord, 1 oz. Grand Marnier, and lime twists. Combine all three liquors in a shaker filled with ice, shake, and strain into a martini glass. Garnish with the lime. Now, heat a little extra Grand Marnier in a saucepan, then light it with a match and pour the flaming liquid into your drink. This hot 'tail, from the Loa Bar at the International House in New Orleans, is a safe 'n' easy version of the Blue Blazer. Can't light the Grand Marnier? Forget about it and enjoy the cocktail anyway. Lit the Grand Marnier, but can't quite pour it into the martini glass? No biggie—dump it down the sink. Lit yourself on fire? Maybe you'd better stick with Shirley Temples.

201

You're Hosting a Summer Lawn Party and Don't Want to Play Bartender

 PUNCHED-UP PIMM'S

"You've just made the perfect summer garden party drink," says inventor and amateur mixologist Chris Holst. "And you won't have to do it again for hours."

MIXOLOGY

1 cup Pimm's No. 1

1 cup vodka

8 cups ginger ale

1 medium cucumber, sliced into rounds

1 orange (temple or valencia is better than navel) sliced into rounds

Freeze a block of ice—preferably in a decorative ring mold. Place the ring in the punch bowl, then pour the Pimm's and vodka over the ice. Add the ginger ale, then the fruit and vegetable, and carry it outside.

You're Watching Sex and the City

 CLASSIC COSMOPOLITAN

Singlehandedly, HBO's *Sex and the City* made vice cool again. In any given episode, you can see Mr. Big holding a rocks glass full of single-malt Scotch, or Steve the ex-bartender swilling a beer, or even Samantha toking up some fine Hawaiian Gold. But the vice of choice in the big, bad, sexy city, of course, is the venerable Cosmo. These ladies pound them like priests pray.

MIXOLOGY

1 oz. vodka

1/2 oz. Cointreau

1 tbsp. lime juice

1 splash cranberry juice

Lime peel

Combine all ingredients in the cocktail shaker. Shake gently. With a steady hand, strain into a martini glass. Fill it right up to the rim. For extra flair, float a curl of lime peel in the center of your drink.

🎲 THE PERFECT DRINKING GAME FOR THIS SITUATION: Turn on any episode of *Sex and the City*—the first few seasons are currently available on VHS and DVD.

Sip your Cosmo whenever:

Carrie types the show's big question.

Carrie wears a ridiculous outfit.

Carrie freaks out/mentions/seems to be thinking about/calls

Mr. Big.

Samantha talks sex.

Miranda complains about something.

Charlotte mentions marriage/babies.

A main character gets lucky (drink twice if it's Samantha).

A main character breaks up with someone or gets dumped.

Stanford makes an appearance.

Finish your drink if:

One of the ladies has a lesbian encounter.

A man is shown wearing no pants.

All four main characters meet and eat brunch.

Carrie swears off Mr. Big for good.

You're Watching a James Bond Flick

We interrupt this regularly formatted item to bring you some shocking news: a Martini—shaken, not stirred—is not always the perfect drink for a romp around the world with Britain's toughest secret agent, 007. Sure, ol' Jimmy sucks down Martinis an awful lot. But he also drinks an astounding variety of other alcoholic beverages, according to an excellent Bond website, "Make Mine a 007" (home.earthlink.net/~atomic_rom/007), run by a mysterious character dubbed the "Minister of Martinis." In fact, in both the films and original novels by Ian Fleming, 007 is far more likely to order a flute of champagne or tumbler of Scotch. Here are some additional findings, right from his secret dossier:

1. Dr. No
MEDIUM–DRY VODKA MARTINI

Bond (played by Sean Connery) kicks off his 30-year—and counting—bender with this Martini, made with Smirnoff. But throughout the course of the movie, he also enjoys some Scotch, red wine, and has an interesting scene involving a bottle of 1955 Dom Perignon.

MIXOLOGY

2 oz. Smirnoff vodka

1/2 oz. dry vermouth

Lemon slice

Shake well with ice and pour into a chilled martini glass.

Garnish with a slice of lemon.

2. Goldfinger

MINT JULEP

This is what Auric Goldfinger offers 007 when he comes knocking on the front door. "It's traditional, yet satisfying," explains Goldfinger. Bond instructs the server: "Sour mash, but not too sweet please."

MIXOLOGY

2 1/2 oz. bourbon	1 tsp. powdered sugar
4–6 mint sprigs	2 tsp. water

Take an old fashioned glass and mix the mint leaves, sugar, and water together. Fill the glass with crushed ice, then add the bourbon. Top with more ice and a sprig of mint.

3. Thunderball
RUM COLLINS

A servant of evil agent Emilio Largo offers Bond one of these little mothers. "Yes, just about that hour, isn't it?" says Bond.

MIXOLOGY

2 oz. light rum

1 tsp. powdered sugar

1 oz. lime juice

Club soda

Orange slice

Combine rum and sugar in a chilled collins glass and stir. Now pour in the lime juice and fill with club soda and ice. Add the orange slice on top.

THE PERFECT DRINKING GAME FOR THIS SITUATION: The rules of "James Bond" couldn't be simpler. During any Bond flick drink twice when someone says "James." Drink twice when someone says "Bond." Drink half of your drink when someone says "James Bond." This game becomes as diabolical as Auric Goldfinger when 007 says: "My name is Bond, James Bond."

Your Dad Just Told You He's Having a Sex Change

 SAM THE CHAM

Not only will it take your mind off the news in a forceful—albeit fizzy—way, this drink is also "girlie" enough to share with Dad. Or Mom. Or whatever you're going to start calling him.

MIXOLOGY

4–5 oz. Champagne

3/4 oz. Chambord raspberry liqueur

Add ice cold Champagne to glass, slowly add chilled Chambord until desired raspberry flavor is achieved, and give it a gentle stir to mix.

You're Taking Your Mom to a Bar

 BLOW JOB

This drink is only appropriate if you're her daughter and your mom hasn't been to a bar in 10 years. The sheer joy of watching Mom be properly mortified is worth the cover charge. And after a while, Mom might start to enjoy Blow Jobs. One friend of mine, Vanessa, claims that she and her mom bonded over Blow Jobs a year ago and their relationship has never been better.

MIXOLOGY

1/2 oz. Bailey's Irish Cream

1/2 oz. Kahlua

Whipped cream

Layer these in a shot glass in this exact order. The rules state that you are not allowed to use your hands to lift this shot to your mouth. Yes, you must wrap your lips around the glass, then whip your head back, downing everything in one shot.

You're About to Turn State's Evidence

 JACK ROSE

About to squeal on the syndicate? Hang on to your kneecaps, avoid tall strangers in overcoats who just want to "talk" to you for a minute, and mix up one of these Dutch courage builders. This cocktail is named for Jack Rose, a gangster who in 1912 sang like a canary about the gangland execution of Herman Rosenthal, who ran a gambling den in Manhattan.

MIXOLOGY

1 1/2 oz. applejack

1 oz. lime juice

1/2 oz. grenadine

Pour everything into an ice-filled shaker. Shake, then strain into a chilled cocktail glass.

You Just Bought a Kate Spade Bag

 BELLINI

A perfectly fussy drink for the perfectly fussy consumer. Bartenders can get downright nasty if you dare substitute anything else for authentic peaches. "A Bellini not made with fresh peach juice is not a Bellini!" admonishes Salvatore Calabrese, London bartender and author of *Classic Cocktails*. Robert Hess, a.k.a. DrinkBoy, also says that "the only true way to make [a Bellini] is with white peach puree." You can lay in your batch of fresh white peaches, peel 'em, and puree the bejesus out of them, or you can try to find "California White Peach Puree," a product of the Perfect Puree Company of Napa Valley. ("This excellent product fits the bill perfectly," says Hess.)

MIXOLOGY

1 oz. white peach puree   5 oz. Champagne

Pour the puree into a Champagne flute, then add the Champagne.

MIX IT RIGHT: You can cheat and make a Quick-Stop Bellini, which is simply 6 oz. Champagne and 1 oz. peach schnapps. But that's just a cheap knock-off.

You're Reading Shakespeare

 LADY MACBETH

This cocktail comes from Joe's Pub in Manhattan's Lower East Side. The bar was named in honor of Joseph Papp, founder of Manhattan's Shakespeare in the Park.

MIXOLOGY

4 oz. Champagne   Lemon twist

4 oz. ruby port

Pour the Champagne into a flute, then add the ruby port. Now leave it alone—you don't mess with the Lady. Garnish with a twist of lemon.

You're Reading Ernest Hemingway

 PAPA DOBLE

Supposedly, old Papa concocted this gem at Sloppy Joe's Bar in Key West, Florida. One might think all the guy did was sit around and invent drink recipes. If Hemingway were alive today, he'd probably be working for T.G.I. Friday's.

MIXOLOGY

2 oz. light rum

2 oz. lime juice

Juice from half a grapefruit

1 dash Maraschino liqueur

Pour the first three ingredients over crushed ice in a highball glass, then float a dash of Maraschino liqueur on top.

MIX IT RIGHT: Hemingway purists might want to try his Death in the Afternoon. Pour 1½ oz. Pernod into a champagne glass, then add chilled champagne until it looks milky. Old Papa himself gave this recipe to the editors of *Esquire* in the 1950s. He suggested that you "drink three or five of these slowly." (We suggest you consider the source of this advice.)

You're Reading Stephen J. Hawking's
The Nature of Space and Time

 BRAIN HEMORRHAGE

All things being equal, if X is traveling into space approaching the speed of light and Y is back on Earth, observing a cat in a box that may or may not be alive depending on whether or not the observer opens the lid, then . . . aw, fuck it.

MIXOLOGY

3 oz. strawberry schnapps

$3/4$ oz. Bailey's Irish Cream

$3/4$ oz. grenadine

Pour over ice, then strain into a shot glass.

⑪ THE PERFECT HANGOVER CURE

> *"Everyone should believe in something. I believe I'll have another drink."*—Unknown

For centuries, writers have grappled with translating the pain of the morning after into words. Dante's *Inferno* comes close. But even that falls short of describing the fresh hell of your body taking its revenge. Perhaps the Norwegians said it best: *jeg har tommermen.* That's the Norwegian phrase for "hangover," and it means: "carpenters in my head."

The trick is not to fight back—because you'll lose—but to bribe your body with sweet nothings, convince it to work with you, not against you, and whisper sweet murmurs that you'll never, ever do anything like this again. If that doesn't work, give these hangover remedies a shot.

When You Wake up Vaguely Hungover

 GET-OUT-OF-JAIL-FREE CARD

Let's face it: A Bloody Mary looks like something Hannibal Lecter would order at a health club. However, every element of this save-your-ass drink does work to make you feel somewhat human again: the vodka will balance out the alcohol in your blood system; the orange juice will help you metabolize the booze faster, the ginger will calm the maelstrom in your stomach, and the cherries contain a certain antioxidant called "anthocyanin," which can relieve pain like aspirin.

MIXOLOGY

1 oz. vodka

4 oz. orange juice

2 oz. ginger ale

Maraschino cherries

Mix liquids with crushed ice in a highball glass and stir. Then garnish with maraschino cherries.

When You're Really Hungover

 ## BULLSHOT

Hemingway used to drink Bloody Marys, but a real man's man would chose a Bullshot, since its base is beef broth, not tomato juice. The Bullshot is the perfect antidote for all the bullshit you put your liver through last night.

MIXOLOGY

2 oz. vodka

2 oz. beef broth or beef
   bouillon

2 dashes Worcestershire
   sauce

1 dash Tabasco sauce

1 tsp. lemon juice

Ground pepper

Lemon wedge

Shake everything except the pepper and lemon wedge with cracked ice and strain into a rocks glass. Now, microwave it until nice and warm, then sprinkle pepper on top and add the lemon. (Prefer it cold? Don't nuke it; simply strain over ice in a rocks glass, then add the pepper and lemon.)

DRINKS TO AVOID IN THIS SITUATION: Don't worry—you'll pretty much be avoiding drinks anyway.

When You're Really, Really Hungover

 PRAIRIE OYSTER

This ages-old remedy is supposed to squash headaches and calm stomachs. Supposedly, this drink was named by a deliriously hungover cowboy, who mumbled something about wanting his "prairie oyster," and the weird name stuck.

MIXOLOGY

1 egg yolk	Ground black pepper
2 tbsp. ketchup	1 dash Worcestershire sauce
Virgin olive oil	1 dash white wine vinegar
Salt	

First, rinse a small wine glass with the oil, then dump the remainder. Moan a little. Now, add the ketchup and egg yolk, without breaking the yolk. Season with the rest of the ingredients. Remind yourself that whatever doesn't kill you makes you stronger. Down it in one gulp.

MIX IT RIGHT: Some recipes call for a jigger of brandy to be added to the mix. Go for it, if you believe that a little more booze will help even you out. It's your stomach.

When You're Hungover and Hungry

 EGGSCELLENT MEDICINE

"Heals two," writes Ted Allen in *Esquire*, which provided this settle-your-tummy breakfast in the January 2000 issue (just in time for the Big Hangover). It was originally whipped up by Allen Sternweiler, former executive chef of Harvest on Huron in Chicago.

MIXOLOGY

5 eggs	1 tsp. minced chives
Salt	2 slices smoked salmon
Ground black pepper	8 slices bacon
3 tbsp. milk	2 slices cheddar cheese
1 tbsp. butter	Dijon mustard
1 tbsp. sour cream	2 English muffins, toasted

Fry the bacon. Whip the eggs with the salt, pepper, and milk. Melt a tablespoon of butter in a frying pan on medium heat, pour in the eggs, and scramble. Just before the eggs are firm, mix in the sour cream and chives. Spread mustard on the muffins and divide the eggs between them. Top with the salmon, bacon, and cheddar.

When You're Hungover Enough to Try Anything

 LOUIE'S BACKYARD CURE

This recipe comes from Louie's Backyard in Key West, as reported by John Mariani in *Playboy*. "Chug it fast and repeat the dosage if your symptoms persist," writes Mariani.

MIXOLOGY

1 oz. Evan Williams Single Barrel bourbon

Raw egg

Tabasco sauce

In a tall glass filled with ice cubes, mix the bourbon, the raw egg, and a few dashes of hot sauce. Good luck.

Other Assorted Hangover Cures

Not scientifically tested by yours truly, but what the hell.

1   "The Bachelor" of swankpad.org says that after "extensive research in Cuba and personal research all over the world," the best possible cure for a hangover is chicken. The Cuban cure involves chicken necks; instead, "The Bachelor" says a nice chicken breast sandwich will suffice.

2   *Ted Shane's Bar Guide* (1950) includes the Hangover Breakfast, which is: a little of the hair of the dog that bit you. A pint of milk. A half-pint of tomato or clam juice. A cup of black coffee sweetened with one teaspoon of "aromatic spirits of ammonia," at which point you should "return to bed and expire." Buddy, I was already gone with the clam juice.

3   Some bleary-eyed folks in Puerto Rico, according to *Bartender Magazine* publisher Ray Foley, recommend rubbing half a lemon under each armpit. Foley also recommends drinking a flat beer left out overnight, or two ounces of Fernet Branca on the rocks.

4   My brother Gregg—a restaurant manager and bartender—recommends some Angostura bitters with soda water when you're feeling hungover and sick as hell. And he's been there quite a few times. Once in my apartment.

5   You might want to rob a jewelry store. Ancient Greeks believed that amethysts had curative powers, which is why their drinking goblets used to be embedded with dozens of the suckers.

6   According to P. T. Elliott's drinking lore book, *100 Proof*, various celebrities had their own hangover cures. Frank Sinatra recommended gin and cream for the morning after. "It's just the ticket, believe me." Roger "The Other James Bond" Moore ate ice cream. Alice Cooper used to blend tuna fish, pistachio ice cream, and milk to ease his personal nightmare. Mike D. from the Beastie Boys says you should get shitfaced again—"Forget the hair-of-the-dog thing; you'll be needing the whole coat." Dean Martin, of course, agrees, recommending that the sufferer "stay drunk."

7   Every now and again, with the appearance of a gibbous moon, somebody comes out with a pre-packaged drug store "hangover cure." These are largely bullshit—and I know from experience. Back in college, my magazine internship boss gave me a bottle and said, "This is going to solve all of your problems."

"What is it?" I asked.

"Hangover relief formula," he replied. "Now listen carefully. I want you to find a party this weekend at school and get wasted. Trashed. Screwed up out of your mind. I want you to have alcohol bleeding from your pores. I want you to destroy large portions of your brain. In fact, I want you to perform the world's first tequila lobotomy."

Actually, he said: "If you have the occasion to use this at school, let me know how it works."

In the interest of journalistic integrity, I set out that very night to see if it worked. I went to a friend's campus apartment and drank a little, not too much, but it was a fun time . . . hey, wassup man i boy . . . why c-can't everybuddy get along in this world . . . THREE MAN! im not drunk . . . IMMM NOT DRUNNKK hey thazz my elbow.

The next morning, I awoke and tried the "hangover relief formula." The label said it was peppermint flavored liquid analgesic/antacid suspension with a mild anti-depressant in a monosaccharide carbohydrate base. I don't know about that. I do know that it tasted like warm, cheap toothpaste mixed with fabric softener. I felt warm and gushy. The room spun around me. Good God, I suddenly needed to vomit.

That was the last time I trusted a magazine editor.

8. In Raymond Chandler's *The Long Goodbye*, private eye Philip Marlowe comes to the realization that he's "looking at life through the mists of a hangover." What does the toughest dick in L.A. do about it? "I decided to kill the hangover. Ordinarily I was not a morning drinker. The Southern California climate is too soft for it. You don't metabolize fast enough. But I mixed a tall cold one this time and sat in an easy chair with my shirt open and pecked at a magazine . . . I was handling the drink carefully, a sip at a time, watching myself."

9. The Official Harvard Student Agencies Bartending Course recommends a sauna or steam bath the next morning, which will boost your circulation (your blood, not social status) and open up some pores.

10. Quit being an atheist.

FURTHER READING

For further reading and mixing and imbibing, these books couldn't come more highly recommended.

The Bon Vivant's Companion or, How to Mix Drinks, by Professor Jerry Thomas (Alfred A. Knopf, 1928). The quintessential mixology guide by the quintessential American bartender.

The Savoy Cocktail Book, by Harry Craddock (1930; updated and expanded in 1999 by Pavilion Books Limited).

Old Waldorf Bar Days, by Albert Stevens Crockett, (Aventine Press, 1931). Subtitle: *With the Cognomina and Composition of Four Hundred and Ninety-One Appealing Appetizers and Salutary Potations Long Known, Admired, and Served at the Famous Big Brass Rail; also, A Glossary for the Use of Antiquarians and Students of American Mores.* And to think—Prohibition wasn't even repealed yet.

My New Cocktail Book, by G. F. Steele (Charles Watson Russell Press, 1934).

Irvin S. Cobb's Own Recipe Book, written by Mr. Cobb for Frankfort Distilleries, Incorporated (1934).

The Fine Art of Mixing Drinks, by David A. Embury (Doubleday & Company, 1946).

The Official Mixer's Manual for Home and Professional Use, by Patrick Gavin Duffy (Perma Giant, 1949).

Bar Guide, by Ted Shane (Gold Medal Books, 1950).

The Esquire Drink Book, edited by Frederic A. Birmingham (Harper & Brothers, 1956).

The ABC of Cocktails (Peter Pauper Press, 1957).

Michael Jackson's Bar & Cocktail Companion (Running Press, 1995).

The Martini Companion: A Connoisseur's Guide, by Gary Regan and Mardee Haidin Regan (Running Press, 1997).

Classic Cocktails, by Salvatore Calabrese (Sterling, 1997).

The Complete Idiot's Guide to Mixing Drinks, by The Players and Alan Axelrod (Alpha Books, 1997).

Bartending for Dummies, by Ray Foley (IDG Books, 1997).

Modern Cocktails & Appetizers, by Martha Gill (Longstreet Press, 1998).

Cocktail: The Drinks Bible for the 21st Century, by Paul Harrington and Laura Moorhead (Viking, 1998).

Atomic Cocktails: Mixed Drinks for Modern Times, by Karen Brooks, Gideon Bosker, and Reed Darmon (Chronicle Books, 1998).

Vintage Cocktails: Authentic Recipes and Illustrations from 1920–1960, by Susan Waggoner and Robert Markel (Stewart, Tabori & Chang, 1999).

The Official Harvard Student Agencies Bartending Course, Third Edition (St. Martin's Griffin, 1999).

100 Proof: Tips and Tales for Spirited Drinkers Everywhere, by P. T. Elliott (Plume, 2000).

Bacchus & Me: Adventures in the Wine Cellar, by Jay McInerney (Vintage, 2000).

Straight Up or On the Rocks: The Story of the American Cocktail, by William Grimes (North Point Press, 2002).

The New American Bartender's Guide, by John J. Poister (New American Library, 1988, updated 2002).

INDEX

For easy reference, here are alphabetical listings of all the drinks—by name and base spirit.

BY BASE SPIRIT

Absinthe

Applejack

Bailey's Irish Cream

Blue Curacao

Brandy

About the Author

Duane Swierczynski is an editor at *Philadelphia Magazine* and has worked as a writer and editor for *Men's Health* and *Details*. He's also the author of *This Here's a Stick-Up: The Big, Bad Book of American Bank Robbery*. He lives and drinks in Philadelphia with his wife, Meredith, and their son, Parker. Did Swierczynski forget to include a perfect drink for a specific occasion? Email the author at duane.swier@verizon.net.

Drinking Buddies

Let's all toast Jason Rekulak, my tireless (and patient) editor, who didn't cut me off when I stayed out way too late. Also, cheers to April White, who served as my official researcher, venturing into strange bars, and even stranger archives in search of booze lore. David Hale Smith has been holding my hair out of my face for about three years now. I'd like to buy a round for everyone at the bar, including David Borgenicht, Matt Madden, Susan Van Horn, Andrea Stephany, Emily Betsch, Erin Slonaker, Loren Feldman, Rich Rys, Gary Goldstein, Greg Clark, Amy Musto, Valentine O'Connor, Thomas Paul, Sr., Paula Mancini, Joe Kita, Jeffery Lindemuth, Ron Geraci, Sasha Issenberg, Hugh Garvey, Chris Moore, Louis Wojciechowski, Courtney Dreslin, and of course, all of my friends and family.

Most of all, a flute of the world's most expensive champagne for my wife Meredith—even though she'd much prefer a $3 bottle of Boone Farm's peach wine. Meredith was pregnant with our boy Parker during the research and writing of this book and couldn't try a single damned thing. (Okay, okay. She did sneak a sip of Vanil Stoli four weeks after the baby was born. The kid never noticed.)

"The whole world is drunk and we're just the cocktail of the moment. Someday soon, the world will wake up, down two aspirin with a glass of tomato juice, and wonder what the hell the fuss is about."

—DEAN MARTIN